"Once upon a time...
he wasn't feeling it anymore."

What's killing romance in America -
And what to do about it.

A guide for the undecided couple.

Jacob Z. Hess, Ph.D.

SWANSEA
— PUBLISHING —

Dedication

To Diana and Jana, and to your beautiful families.

Also, to couples now and in the future who would be unbelievably happy together, if only they could see each other clearly and completely - as the persons they *actually are*.

"Sometimes the greatest journey is the distance between two people."
- The Painted Veil (2006)

Preface

I was duped!

The lighting, the props and the set...the voiceovers, airbrushing and costumes. Day by day, the scripts told me what I *should* feel and how I *should* be acting in relation to love and romance. Line-by-line, I was guided in how it's all *supposed to be*.

Funny enough, I thought it was real!

And I'm not the only one. The dominant American narrative of romance has swept most of us off our feet. Locked in the embrace of this story, our collective experience of love and intimacy continues to be shaped and molded in directions that repeatedly depart from what we really want.

Among otherwise smart, successful and happy individuals, Barabara Whitehead writes, there is "a widespread sense of anxiety and confusion" when it comes to romance - a "feeling that something had gone wrong in their love lives."[i]

After years of my own relationship heartache, I was hurting and deeply perplexed. Why had dating become so hard and love so complicated? And why did I keep walking away from amazing possibilities?

In the middle of my Ph.D. program at the Unversity of Illinois, I started interviewing other singles in different circumstances, searching for some answers. Long before, I had started gathering relevant commentary, articles and books about love and romance from as many perspectives as I could find.

After nearly 15 years of exploring, I don't claim to have discovered any dramatic secrets. But I have felt profoundly taught and changed by the stories and insights I've heard. This book is my attempt to share what I've learned and come to love over the years.

I still have plenty to learn, and if you're willing to share your story, I would love to listen (see www.not feelingit.org). In the meanwhile, if anything I've gathered can be helpful to you - married or single, happy or currently baffled as much as I was, I would be thrilled.

-Jzh, 10/31/13

Acknowledgments

My deepest thanks to Monique Tenaya Moore, who has read multiple drafts, helped with interviews, and cheered my heart along to the finish line. To my brother and research assistant, Daniel Hess, a huge thanks for giving so much of yourself in conducting 20 interviews, reviewing several drafts and filming a fabulous video.

Appreciations to others who reviewed the text at various stages: Jake Stauber, Julianne Zollinger, Lisa Fraser, Aaron Gale, James Keller, Russell Grover, Jessica Moon - and to Mike and Erica Nutting for hosting my writing retreat.

A heartfelt thanks to the many loved ones whose stories are inextricably tied to my own and who have shared defining moments of this journey with me, including sisters Mary E. P. Hess and Katie Hess, brothers Elijah Hess and John Thompson, and cousins Nate Zollinger, Trevor Davis, Natalie (Zollinger) Reber, Stephanie (Zollinger) Stauber and Brenda Hale.

To my lovely sister Julia Rose Hess, gratitude for sharing the most painful times of all and for eventually showing her older brother what it means to love and trust with everything we've got. To Alicia Williams, for teaching me about a love way bigger than Self. And to my angel brother Sam, who has kept his promises.

Above all, I thank those who have taught me what it means to truly love: my father and hero Paul Hess, my dearly-missed angel mother Martha Zollinger, my beloved grandfather Milton J. Hess, and again, my forever sweetheart, Monique.

Table of Contents

Introduction

Megan's excited trembling was visible, as she told us: "I met someone!" Home for Christmas break, she recounted to our group of friends the dizzying tale of her autumn romance. Her man, Ryan, was home with his family in another state for a couple of days, but proof of his existence lay snug on her finger - a ring glistening like a fairy tale come true. She could hardly wait for the holiday break to be over so she could see him again.

One week later, Megan appeared with an ashen face. "What's wrong? What happened? Why are you?...." In broken voice, she explained that Ryan had just stopped calling - with no explanation. Initially confused, she soon became fearful that something had happened. Was he hurt or maybe in an accident? In a near frantic state, Megan finally heard Ryan's voice on the other end of the phone. "What happened?!" she asked: "Why haven't you called?"

It turns out that Ryan was still safely enjoying the holidays at his family's cabin. But something unfortunate *had* happened: *his feelings had changed.* "I'm sorry, Megan," he said, "I just don't feel like I used to...it's just not the same for me anymore."

Ten days before, Ryan had held Megan close as they shared tender goodbyes at the airport. One month ago, he insisted that he couldn't live without her. But all that had changed now, because after all...he wasn't feeling it anymore.

If this true story deserves any label, it would not be "unique." One man reflected on a recent break-up: "I have strong feelings initially - buying her flowers, saying sweet nothings, dedicating songs to her, wanting to put a smile on her face all the time, wanting to help her be happier - to the next minute nothing. Off immediately, like a light switch. It's weird, I just lose it."

Another guy said: "Initially, I felt a crush and attraced...but there would come a point where I just felt nothing anymore; I just had no affection for them. They were just like anyone else."

Another told me: "After 2-3 months, my heart would start to dry up toward that person. I would let her down as gently as I could."

Another said: "My affection would die over time after the initial excitement of dating someone wore off. I have suddenly changed a number of times."[1]

And another: "I broke up with a wonderful girl three times because the bubbling feeling had faded."

And one more: "I would go from first kissing her when things were new and fresh, and writing in my journal that I thought I would marry her [to] then 3 weeks later, I would break up with her."

One woman told me: "We date, things are great, we're happy, good to go - then it just drops off." Another woman said "it was always super exciting and butterflies and firework - and always around six months, he would lose interest. And I would get clingy and try to convince him to stay."

So obviously this must be a guy issue alone, right? Not so fast! One woman described breaking up four times with her boyfriend "because one day I would all of a sudden stop feeling it." The next day, she said, "I would think, why did I do that? I really liked him":

Each time I thought it was starting to work, I would lose that feeling and just start to feel anxious. Friends would tell me to break up and I assumed that was the only answer. It was torture to have that conversation each time. There was no explanation to give him except that I didn't feel enough. After the last time, I cried for several days. I really wanted it to work.

She really wanted it to work. He really wanted it to work. We were all *really hoping* this one would turn out...but it doesn't. Despite heroic and earnest efforts, too often grand possibilities disintegrate right before our eyes.

I would know. No one has betrayed grander possibilities than I. No matter how lovely, how fun and how remarkable she was, something was missing. It wasn't enough. She wasn't enough. And I was absolutely paralyzed.

---

[1] To make the numerous interview quotes more readable and accessible, ellipses that indicate deletions have been removed. Otherwise, they reflect verbatim what was shared during interviews [with additions appearing in brackets]. For those interested in the original quotes with attached numerical codes, I'm happy to provide a more academic version of this manuscript.

Romance hijacked

In the ruins of past relationships, we end up saying something like: *'It didn't work out'* or *'It just wasn't right'* or *'It really wasn't there.'*[2]

And that definitely could all be true. But does saying these things settle the matter for anyone? Could something more be going on?

I certainly thought so. After years of painful dating experiences, the confusion and heartache were too much. So I did what qualitative researchers do to cope with life: I started interviewing.

When I began listening to people's stories and first noticed the theme of transient, up-and-down romance, I assumed I was observing a distinctive pattern in my own, local faith community. Then I had lunch with my pagan neighbor - a bachelor guy who worshipped Odin and had also recently broken up with his girlfriend. And what did he tell me?

The *same* things I'd been hearing from everyone else! He said, "I basically stopped caring. I went from really, really, really caring, to just walking away. I just stopped talking with her - she didn't understand why. That's what happens to me. All of a sudden, I just turn it off."

Older and younger, religious and not, liberal and conservative - the pattern held consistent across interview participants.[3] Whether people were married, cohabiting, or single - the sudden vanishing act of romance was stunning.

So my sophisticated research question became something like this: *What in tarnation is going on?* Why do romantic relationships seem so increasingly transitory, fleeting and elusive these days - and what, if anything, can be done about it?

---

[2] In cases of imaginary or generalized dialogue that doesn't refer to an actual book or interview participant, single quotation marks are used throughout. I favor this as a way to differentiate quotes with valid sources from other useful, creative extrapolations.

[3] While these patterns are remarkably cross-cutting, no interviews were conducted with couples in the LGBT community. Given the divergence of public views around sexual orientation, a separate manuscript in preparation will explore the implications of these contested narratives.

Let the hypotheses begin

I'm definitely not the only one asking these questions. Researchers, social commentators and every bachelor's grandmother in the nation are all wondering what's going on with romance in America. These questions became a kind of hobby to my own sweet mother over the years: 'I play the piano, do crossword puzzles...and try to figure out why my son's relationships never work out.'

So what's the answer?

#1. Just-not-working-hard-enough. One theory, especially popular among parents, focuses on the right amount of work and effort needed for a successful relationship. One person I interviewed asserted with confidence, "An individual does not end up alone and single without a certain dose of complacency," suggesting that those without partners were just "not trying" hard enough. From this view, laziness is the primary problem among singles, from this view.

If so, then maybe people just need a good kick in the pants to get them moving? One parent I interviewed told me, "I just want to knock them both over the head" and "tell them to get on with it."

It's true that increasing numbers of young adults show little or no interest in long-term relationships.[1] One man in his late twenties said he was "in no hurry to get married."[2] Another guy wanted to travel and "hang out with his bro's" for awhile before getting serious with anyone.[3]

While most people don't want to rush into marriage, large majorities of individuals still envision making that commitment at some point.[4] And many of these have worked pretty hard to get there...alas!

#2. Too-darn-picky. If the first explanation has the most votes among the parent demographic, the second candidate is running strong with grandparents and other relatives: 'Kids these days wouldn't know a good thing if it hit 'em in the face!'

According to this theory, individual pickiness is the smoking gun at the mass singleness crime scene. If everyone broadened their expectations, happy, lasting relationships would result...and soon!

And again, this certainly can be a legitimate factor. One woman said, "I have friends who can make a list of **35** things they want....They haven't been in a serious relationship for years....Even when guys are attractive to them, they are not good enough for them." One older bachelor told me, "I'm a nose person" - going on to detail the particular kind of schnoz crucial to identifying the woman of his dreams.

In a later chapter, we'll discuss how our scope of attraction can narrow to an almost ridiculous range. The question here, is whether pickiness alone can explain all the turbulence in romance these days.

Let me check...Nope!

#3. Maybe-you-should-talk-to-someone. A third theory gains points for sounding especially sophisticated, using terms that sound vaguely psychological, such as 'commitment phobia' and 'avoidance issues.'

For a guy past a certain age, you're almost guaranteed to hear the all-purpose 'he's just got *issues.*' One married individual said, "If you're not in a relationship and older, you've got to have issues. There's *got* to be something going on."

The common focus of all three hypotheses is worth noticing: namely, establishing what is *internally wrong* with single individuals. Lazy. Picky! Sick? From so many directions, in so many forms, this notion can become irresistible - including to singles themselves.

Just messed up?

One of the most common things in interviews with singles was this: "There is no way to not feel, 'why am I not good enough?'"

Or this: "I have wondered constantly at times, 'what's wrong with me?'"

Or this: "You start to wonder what's wrong with you, and why you aren't married."

It goes without saying that this kind of message has the potential to make a hard situation *even harder.* After describing a friend who went through "long spells of not being asked out," one man said this "kind of jacked with her psyche a little bit." Another individual described many of her older single girlfriends falling into depression.

But if these people were just working a little harder, being a little less picky and maybe seeing their therapist more regularly, couldn't we nip this in the bud? Or maybe the next make-over or dating technique would be enough to find the right person?

That's the message of the many movies depicting "quirky, lovelorn women who, after metamorphoses, emerge 'fixed' and finally suitable for marriage"...or the lists of relationship "don'ts" and tips, with titles like "*Stop Sabotaging Your Relationships*" and "*The Ten Stupid Things You Do to Chase Away Prince Charming.*"[5]

Maybe the magazines are right after all, to blame women for being either "too giving or too self-absorbed, too needy or too independent, too demanding or not demanding enough, too emotionally controlling or too emotionally out of control."[6] "I feel myself beginning to cave" one woman writes, "Who am I kidding? I can't refute this arsenal of why-I'm-dateless data. I guess they're right....I'm too needy, too independent, too crazy, or too reclusive. Too emotional, too cerebral, too passive, or too domineering. Too something...All I have to do is identify and correct the character flaw (or two or three) that repels the good ones, and then I, too, will find Mr. Right."[7]

Or maybe not?

After meeting literally hundreds of single guys and girls who are remarkably mentally healthy, who are working very hard at dating, and who are keeping their expectations open, I can't help but ask myself - what if there is nothing fundamentally *wrong* with those who don't happen to be partnered yet?

Welcome to the Petri dish

In my professional work researching depression, I've arrived at the same question. It's easy for those facing the intense pain of depression to also conclude there must be something deeply wrong internally - 'maybe I'm just messed up?'[8]

While internal factors can always play a role, if they get all the attention, we can end up missing out on the larger picture of what's really happening. Have you ever heard of the video game Sim City? In this popular game, you are the all-powerful ruler, the King or Queen of your own civilization. With endless money and power, you guide how this society works in every detail, with the sole responsibility of creating conditions that will allow citizens to live, work and be happy.

In my depression recovery class, we flip this game on its head - instead imagining that you now have a sinister agenda as all-powerful ruler. Rather than creating society conditions that cultivate prosperity and well-being, participants scheme up a new culture that will effectively incubate widespread emotional problems - like a gigantic Petri dish: What kind of things will people eat or drink? How are they entertained? What kind of pace of life do they keep up? How are their relationships and community connections?

Once we've created a depression-inducing culture, maybe we're ready to take it to the next level. What would we need to do to make sure a society stifles and muffles romantic progress, ensuring that long-term love fizzles as much as possible? How could we work towards people no longer being attracted to normal human beings in the first place. Any good ideas?

I've been asking people this question and collecting answers on my blog.[9] My favorite answers so far:

- "For starters, I would work to make sure people didn't feel well physically - (e.g., discouraging exercise or drinking water, encouraging people to eat something that's not real food, etc)."
- "Make sure people always have something to do (besides being with other people). Always!"
- "I would get my people in a pattern of always getting what they want - and quick!"

It doesn't take long playing this pretend game before an obvious realization hits: The point of the game is that this is no game.

In the case of depression, researchers from Clark University and the University of Washington recently suggested that multiple risk factors in our society have created a current atmosphere that is partially "giving birth" to depression:

> The growing number of depressed people can be attributed to a "depressogenic society" - a society that places many of its members at risk for developing depression...You may be living in a society that makes you more prone to depression on a number of levels.[10]

7

A kind of literal *social climate change* is happening throughout the world right now. So how about with relationships?

"For the first time in history," Naomi Wolf writes, youth are growing up with their "earliest sexual imprinting deriv[ing] not from a living human being." For the last couple of decades, she continues, "the sexuality of children has begun to be shaped in response to cues that are no longer human...imprinted with a sexuality that is mass-produced."[11]

If this is true, would it impact romantic relationships? In 2007, the American Psychological Association released a report summarizing the research studies examining the sexualization of girls in America. Right in the middle of that report is the following statement: "Exposure to narrow ideals of female attractiveness may make it difficult for some men to find an acceptable partner or to fully enjoy intimacy with a female partner."[12] The report also notes, "many individuals have become uncomfortable with 'real bodies.'"[13]

People have become so accustomed to high levels of visual novelty and stimulation, other experts note, that they're often "unable to focus" on real human beings[14] – reflecting "eroding individual apprecia-tion of the unaltered human form"[15] where "suddenly a normal [per-son's] body looks abnormal."[16]

Welcome to the U.S.A., 2013! This is our society - the soup we're all swimming in.

Romantic upheaval

Something is rotten in the state of modern romance. This is the conclu-sion from a veritable chorus of social commentators and scholarly research[17] now raising concern with the "pervasive sense of romantic discontent"[18] experienced by so many and highlighting a cultural "shake-up of love's playing board that no one could have foreseen."[19] Dr. Barbara Whitehead, from Rutgers University, writes that the world of romance is "currently undergoing profound change," citing a "historical upheaval in the long-established mating system" wherein "social forces have changed the timetable and course of love."[20] And historian Stephanie Coontz writes:

The current rearrangement of both married and single life is in fact without historical precedent...Everywhere relations between men and women are undergoing rapid and at times traumatic transformation. In fact...*the relations between men and women have changed more in the past thirty years than they did in the previous three thousand.*[21]

If it's true that these cultural shifts are happening and leaving their mark on our minds, our hearts, and our relationships, then maybe it's time to broaden the conversation about romance. Maybe individuals need something more than pep talks, new-fangled theories of love or more clever tips to extract commitment from the person of their dreams. Maybe surgical enhancements, more trips to the gym or upping our dating average alone won't get to the bottom of this either.

After spending years listening to hundreds of personal stories about romantic relationships, I'm convinced of at least one thing: All this heart-break, sorrow and confusion in romance is not just about people being messed up or personally deficient or simply lacking the skills to 'win at the dating game.' Instead, it seems clear to me that in hundreds of different ways, beautiful individuals and couples are being *messed with* by a larger culture that is profoundly confused when it comes to romance itself.

When it comes to romance problems, I believe it's time to expand our attention beyond individual deficiencies alone to exploring more seriously the cultural landscape around us - the society we're experiencing every day. If we do so, maybe we can learn to navigate this culture better and perhaps even fundamentally change our relationship to it.

Understanding the complexities of culture, however, is no easy task. Among the many methods used, my own preference as a researcher is to go down to the basic building blocks of experience - exploring a unit of analysis that takes into account all levels of complexity: context, feeling, thoughts, action, timing and a thousand other variables.

And what is that? As Muriel Rukeyser once said, on the most fundamental level, the universe is "made of *stories*, not of atoms."[22] Within any individual story can be found a wealth of insight into the lived experience of any cultural moment or situation. At the same time, stories also hold a power in shaping this same life. More than simply telling stories, then, we inevitably come to *live them out.*[23]

The exploration that follows is about a story - yours and mine. A story about beauty, love, romance, and The Feeling.[4] In the chapters ahead, we'll get on our hands and knees and look more closely at the cultural stories we are *all* living out to some degree. In the first chapter, we dive into the most common way romance is often talked about and "narrated." In the subsequent four chapters, we'll then explore specific consequences of that narrative for our experience of romance – including the ensuing burden felt by many couples (Chapter 2), the drivenness of our decision-making (Chapter 3), the maddening levels of indecision (Chapter 4), and the diminishing levels of affection seemingly all around us (Chapter 5).

After considering this fall-out from the dominant narrative of romance, we'll then ask the obvious: Is there another way? In the second half of the book, we'll begin seriously flirting with another suitor who is proposing quite a different romance. After walking through that mind-shift in Chapter 6, we spend the final four chapters doing the same thing we did earlier: discussing what this narrative itself might mean for romance itself. From lightened expectations (Chapter 7), to expanded degrees of freedom, commitment and love (Chapters 8-10) - trust me: the consequences couldn't be more profound.

So that's the plan. I don't know about you, but I'm tired of seeing beautiful relationships and amazing possibilities hijacked. If there's a way out of this current cultural love-madness, then I want to find out!

---

[4] Unconventional capitalization is also used throughout as a way to further punctuate, emphasize and externalize certain elements of the larger discourse on romance - especially those elements that have largely dropped out of public awareness and those that deserve to be surfaced, discussed and thought about a whole lot more.

Part One:

Falling in Love with a Story

"A well-thought-out story doesn't need to resemble real life. Life itself tries with all its might to resemble a well-crafted story." - Isaac Babel

Chapter 1. Romance 101: How It's Supposed To Be

"You were the reason for my existence; to adore you for me was religion...a love...that gave light to my life...without your love I will not live." - Carlos Almarán

"So how is this experience of true love and romance *supposed to be?*" Kind of sounds like a dumb question, no? You know, the kind a teacher asks when the answer is obvious to everyone. Let's be honest. Don't we already all know how love is Supposed To Be?

Knock my socks off, please

Robert Johnson, a therapist who specialized for decades in the psychology of romantic love, writes that true love has come to be defined by a mutual adoration of "overwhelming intensity."[1] A central message of much contemporary pop music, one study concluded, was that true love brings with it pleasures that are "virtually infinite."[2]

You know what they mean: "I did not live until today. How can I live when we are parted?"; being with you is a "breathless delight,"[3] with "every sight" of you bringing "not a quiet happiness, but unearthly bliss."[4]

We're not talking about a delightful moment here. This is being head-over-heels. Swept-off-feetness. Crazyness. Overwhelm. What the French call "le click." According to the dominant story-line, *this* is the litmus test and threshold for determining true love: breathless, irrational desire.

This has also become the relationship ideal for which so many of us are striving, whether consciously or unconsciously. "There was no point in going on a second date if there wasn't a strong attraction on the first," one woman writes. "I expected to be dazzled."[5] One man quoted a movie line, "If you haven't fallen deeply in love, you haven't lived at all," explaining how that line became a "template" for him and galvanized an expectation that the right person would "knock my socks off and [I would] be totally enthralled from the beginning."

What we may realize is that *it wasn't always like this.* Historians place the formation of this expectation for romantic bliss back to a particular period in the 11-13th century in southern France, where an ideal of courtly love arose. In this cultural aspiration, a brave knight sought to "worship" a fair lady as his inspiration and the *"symbol of all beauty and perfection."*[6] This love was intended to fill the emptiness and void in other areas of life, with passion embraced as a source of meaning, wholeness and fulfillment in a world that felt increasingly empty.

Empty, that is, without The Feeling!

Now and forever

The right person then, will sweep us off our feet and "enthrall" us "from the beginning." Notice the stipulation: right from the *beginning!* "You know if it's right immediately," another man explained. Attraction is thus expected to happen "right away," reflecting what the philosopher Shopenhauer called "the wholly immediate, instinctive attraction."[7]

In addition to happening right away, this intensity of feeling is also expected to show remarkable staying-power and to endure throughout a relationship and throughout a life span. Indeed, what used to be understood as the "special prerogative and province of the young" is now held up as a "romantic privilege" available to all.[8]

The same romantic feelings anticipated as emerging suddenly, are thus also expected to demonstrate a sublime constancy. "If human love ever wanes," another notes, "then it wasn't love in the first place."[9] In one study, 65% of people surveyed reported believing that "the intense passion of the first stages, if it is real, will last, or it should last, forever."[10]

Against this expectation, any vacillation or shifting of romantic feelings can be hard to justify. One woman writes about gradually developing attraction during an engagement that sometimes felt like a "bumpy rollercoaster." "For quite a few months after my wedding," she continued:

> I was ashamed at my courting story with Jason. Because our love for each other developed over some rocky terrain and we both experienced some bouts of serious doubt I felt our relationship was somehow less than the relationships that seemed to follow a more linear path, with almost immediate attraction, blissful dating and a glorious engagement.

If feelings do change, of course, we expect they will grow into something larger and more overwhelming. Anything less than this may be taken as a sign that true love doesn't currently exist, or never existed in the first place.

No one else

Overwhelming. Immediate. Unchanging. What else? "You want to be with her all the time," one man said, "I've heard from people who've been in love that that's what they feel."

Another sign of true love, a man told me, is "not being interested in anyone else." He explained, "If I'm still attracted to other girls in my head, maybe I'm not ready to commit to this other girl."

Did you catch that? The idea is this: before you commit completely to someone, you *must* see this person as the most attractive person you have ever met - or *will* meet! That means you better make sure there's *nothing* you don't like. After all, how else can you have a lasting relationship?

Super relationships

As you begin to see, we're not merely looking for a nice companion or a good match; we're looking for much, much more. Some people call this a "soul mate," as in those annoying magazines at the store (e.g., "The Secrets of Soul Mate Love"). Nearly 90% of people in one survey agreed that this kind of a soul mate was "waiting for you somewhere out there," and an even higher percentage (94%) indicate that this kind of profound connection is their highest priority in a spouse: "you want your spouse to be your soul mate, first and foremost." [11]

In this way, we aspire for some kind of a "Super Relationship" - reflecting all our dreams in one package deal. And who wouldn't want this kind of perfect union and intimacy? Maybe it's crazy to consider anything less?

Maybe. Maybe not. Remember that this level of expectation for romantic partners hasn't been around forever. It was a couple of hundred years after the courtly love of France that the philosopher Rousseau first asserted that "a single human being" could be "experienced as embodying the greatest good and be worthy of the sort of love that was formerly reserved for God." [12]

The idea began to spread across Europe - with the French population by the mid-1800s beginning to speak of "marriage by fascination." In one man's letter to his girlfriend in the late 1800s, he wrote, "I breathe by you; I live by you." [13]

Over time, a deeply held cultural ideal emerged - namely, that in the intimacy of romance could be found answers to some of our deepest, most profound needs. In addition to bringing people together, this kind of intense love was understood to be unchanging over time, with couples expected to "maintain their ardor until death do them part," writes historian Stephanie Coontz. Regarding these "unprecedented goals for marriage," she continues, "Never before in history had societies thought that such a set of high expectations about marriage was either realistic or desirable." [14]

For many, then, falling deeply in love came to be anticipated as the central transcendent experience of life, an "all powerful solution to the problem of finding meaning, security and happiness in life." [15] This was the kind of uplift and self-fulfillment, Coontz continues, "that the previous generation had sought in religious revivals." [16] This was "what we had always longed for," Johnson adds - namely, "a vision of ultimate meaning and unity - suddenly revealed to us in the form of another human being." [17]

While some form of romance has been valued by cultures throughout history (from ancient Greece and the Roman Empire, to ancient Persia and feudal Japan) the difference today, one scholar concludes, is that our modern Western society is the "first" and "only culture in history" that has come to expect its presence "all the time" as the "basis of our marriage and love relationships" and the marker of "true love"[18]

So what does all this mean for actual relationships? If this is what (and how) we decide romantic love is *Supposed To Be*, does it really make that much of a difference in our lives and relationships? I'd love to hear what you think about that!

Chapter 2. Heavy:
Romance Overloaded

Expectation is the root of all heartache. - Gautama Buddha[1]

Intense. Immediate. Constant. All-consuming. What could possibly go wrong in pursuing a romance that fits all these criteria?

When I set off to find this kind of romance for myself, I certainly wasn't anticipating any problems. After all, isn't this the dream we're all seeking?

Something happened along the way, however, that made me realize something was fishy - not with me, or with my hopes for love - but with the story in my head *about* love.

So what's up? No one's arguing with romance here. We all want it. And we can certainly have it.

But what this romantic love looks like exactly, and what it means to pursue it, are unique in our current culture when compared with previous human history. In the next four chapters, we'll take a closer look at the details of how this new-fangled story of romance plays out for actual relationships. As you will see, the consequences of this narrative are not what you might expect.

Please meet my demands

Intense. Immediate. Constant. All-consuming. If that's the love we're going after and committed to - well, what next?

Well, of course, some of us find it. And that's great! The consuming intensity of romantic love can be one of the sweetest experiences of life. And it's a no-brainer that we want it in our lives.

The question we're exploring here is why is that experience has become so elusive, so hard to find, *and* so hard to keep for so many of us these days? We're hot on the trail of an answer once we've grasped the larger storyline shaping our romantic pursuits.

So let's cut right to the chase. You ready? In broad daylight, here's the first consequence of our favorite story-of-romance in a nutshell: normal human beings (and relationships between normal human beings) cannot and will not live up to *other-worldly, super-human expectations*. Period!

Unless you're secretely living as a super-hero among us, you are one of the mere mortals living on earth. And every earthling I know happens to struggle *with something*. Relationships between humans (good relationships) can therefore be challenging and messy sometimes.

We're all aware of this, of course. What we may not be aware of is *just how much messier* relationships can become when we saddle them with the story of romance explored in the previous chapter.

And, of course, that's precisely what we're doing. As summarized by philosopher Simon May at King's College in London:

> We expect love to be a...journey for the soul, a final source of meaning and freedom...a key to the problem of identity, a solace in the face of rootlessness...a redemption from suffering, and, a promise of eternity. Or all of these at once. In short: *love is being overloaded.*[2]

By requiring love to reflect "superhuman qualities" May continues, we force relationships to "labor under intolerable expectations," ultimately "demanding from the loved one far more than they can possible be."[3] Stastistical studies of committed couples have confirmed a measurable increase in emotional expectations for romantic relationships over recent decades.[4]

Have you ever felt any of your own relationships weighed down by some of the expectations we've been exploring? At the time, how did you and your partner make sense of that heaviness? Did those demands contribute to that relationship ending? How do you think that relationships would had been different if those expectations and demands could have been lifted?

It's become increasingly common, as Robert Johnson elaborates, to believe "that this mortal human being has the responsibility for making our lives whole, keeping us happy, making our lives meaningful, intense and ecstatic."[5] The right person is thus "expected to meet virtually impossible expectations." another notes - with a wife, husband or intimate partner "supposed to be gorgeous, a best friend, a superb financial contributor...sexy, and a marvelous parent" and the relationship a "fulfillment of all core needs."[6]

She's out there!

Wow! Who wouldn't want that? A person and relationship to meet all my core needs. Sign me up!

No wonder we keep searching. One older bachelor hadn't found a lasting relationship for many years, but his mother kept reassuring him to "keep waiting for that perfect girl." So he did.

With each new relationship, though, he kept finding "something wrong with her." But when he met Kelly, he told her, "For the first time, I've met someone that I can't find anything wrong with."

Does that make your heart go pitter-patter...or not? Try out this thought experiment for a minute: Think of all the couples you currently know personally. Then imagine both partners going through a flashy new romance training that effectively persuaded each of them to focus exclusively on the question, 'are all my needs being met in this relationship'?

So here's the question: how many of these couples would stay together? For myself, I'm not sure I would know many intact couples at all!

Of course, this is much more than a thought experiment for many of us. It's our lives! As discussed earlier, thanks to the cultural petri dish all around us, we have been well trained on a variety of levels: 'true' beauty, passionate attraction, and romantic perfection itself. Best-selling author Elizabeth Gilbert writes:

> Contemporary Americans have the grandest, and most outsized expectations about love of any people who have ever lived at any time on earth. We are *completely* infatuated of the idea of soul-matehood, and finding someone who is our absolutely perfect match....[We] want it all...and we live in a culture where we are constantly promised that you can *have*

it all and you can have it tomorrow and you can have it in red, and you can have six of them.[7]

This tendency is clearly not exclusive to one gender. In their search for a "perfect blend of selves,"[8] one author noted that many women "hold a fantasy that their future mate must be perfectly balanced. He'll be a best friend, a high earner, a sexual athlete, and a good housekeeper."[9]

When asked what important qualities they were waiting to find in the right man, a group of women shared these answers with another author conducting interviews: "Even if he's nice and smart and attractive, I can't be with someone boring," one woman said. "Exactly," another followed, "[and] they have to be smart in an interesting way. They have to be curious." "Curious, but not earnest," a third woman interjected, "they have to be a little edgy." "But not too edgy," said the first woman. "They have to be normal. But just not boring."[10]

Some of these same women went on to share a list of dealbreakers for past relationships that had ended. One woman said, "He thought it was funny to make up strange words, like 'fabulosa.' He did this a lot - and in public, too. Once he said to someone at a party, 'Being a doctor isn't just one fabulosa after another' and I was so embarrassed. I broke up with him the next day." Another woman said, "He loved me too much. I felt like he was too much of a puppy dog, always looking at me with those adoring eyes. I wanted more of a manly man."[11]

One man spoke of a sense from women he knows that they "want true love but you'd better be this tall and make this much money - and not have bad moods or be a real person, either."[12]

Another woman reported:

> I look back and think of many good friends that I never saw as potential relationships simply because I didn't feel like I do when I watch *Pride and Prejudice*. These were good guys that had the qualities I was looking for, and whose company I really enjoyed. I am surprised now that I never even thought to give any of them a chance, especially when they really had what I need.

Why would we ignore someone who may have what we need? In some cases, maybe it's not about what we really need anymore. Maybe we're searching for something else.

The body project

Between 2004 and 2006, scholars from Harvard University and the London School of Economics conducted a study of how women across the globe viewed their own attractiveness and beauty. During this time, they surveyed 4,100 women ages 18 to 64, from 13 countries, including Argentina, Brazil, Canada, France, Italy, Japan, Netherlands, Portugal, United Kingdom, United States, Spain, Australia and New Zealand. One of the central findings was that women rated their own "beauty" and "physical attractiveness" as *one and the same*, with ideas of beauty and physical attractiveness "largely synonymous" and "interchangeable." The researchers summarize: "It appears that the word 'beauty' has - in many ways - become functionally defined as 'physical attractiveness.'"[13]

The attraction many of us are seeking in our ideal mates, then, has often come to essentially mean being attracted *to someone's body*. Once again, this has clearly not always been the case historically. According to Plato, the pursuit of beauty centered around seeking one who embodied goodness, truth and one who brought us to harmonious completion. In 1913, *Webster's Dictionary* defined beauty as "properties pleasing the eye, the ear, the intellect, the aesthetic faculty or the moral sense."

But one hundred years later, the researchers note, our default definition of beauty has "shriveled pitifully [with] the contributions of the ear, the intellect, the broader aesthetic faculty or the moral sensibilities [largely] gone." In its place is a view of beauty almost entirely visual.[14] Studies now show that *both* young men and women place a much higher value on physical attractiveness and sexiness in a mate than in years past.[15]

Caring about physical attraction, of course, is only natural, and not a problem. What we're talking about here is a level of preoccupation with the physical that arises to something blatantly unnatural. One woman spoke of being "constantly aware of where others are in the room and whether or not they notice you...You walk into a party thinking, 'Am I wearing too much makeup? Were these pants a good choice? Do I look like I'm trying too hard? I hope they think I look hot!'?" According to a Northwestern University study, this kind of constant self-checking contributes to poor mental health, with one study finding women looking in the mirror 70 times a day, on average.[16]

The historical change in this level of preoccupation is dramatic. Based on analyses of women's diaries from 1830 to the present, Joan Brumberg, a professor of history at Cornell University, discovered a striking shift in the way young women view themselves. Before World War I, women rarely mentioned their bodies as having anything to do with their own personal identity. Becoming a better person meant paying less attention to the self, giving more assistance to others, and gaining more education. In 1892, for instance, one young girl wrote, "Resolved: not to talk about myself or feelings. To think before speaking. To work seriously. To be self restrained in conversation and actions. Not to let my thoughts wander. To be dignified. Interest myself more in others."[17] Brumberg notes that in spite of other serious problems in that era, women of the time were largely focused on inner beauty, good deeds and guarding personal integrity.

By contrast, private diaries of American adolescent girls of this century reflect an increasingly consistent preoccupation with the body as the centerpiece of self-improvement. Rather than a vehicle for the pursuit of other things, finessing and sculpting the body has now become commonly regarded as the primary task at hand, even an "all-consuming project."[18]

Meeting someone with just the right physical features, in turn, can become a project of its own: "Men would approach me because they saw something in me that matched a fantasy they had" one woman wrote. She added, "I knew that the right man would love me *as I was*, and yet I could not imagine being loved that way from day one."[19]

In pivoting from good works to good looks as the highest pursuit of female perfection,[20] actions and behavior come to matter much less in our judgments. As one person said, "anything goes, as long as you don't have thunder thighs."[21]

All right, fellow earthlings, is this really the best we can do?

Narrowing beauty

Of course it's not. Of course there are better ways.

'Wait a minute,' you're thinking. 'Are you telling me physical attraction *isn't* important? That we should stop caring about how the body looks?'

Absolutely not. Rather than questioning physical attraction itself - what we're taking a look at here is one particular view of beauty: a beauty story almost entirely consumed by the physical.

But it's not just that. You see, even if we limited ourselves to the body, there's also a wide range of physical attractions possible. But in this dominant cultural story of love, we're being encouraged to embrace one *narrowly-defined type* of physical attraction as well. With precision any marketer would be proud of, certain body types have been branded as "must-have."

Want to maximize sex appeal? Better stick to the brand guidelines: ideal size, color, smell - all laid out in unmistakable detail. "Sensuality equals beauty" one author notes, "that's what people today are learning."[22] Although not to the extent of female standards,[23] physical and sexual expectations for men are also in the process of narrowing.

The story then, is one of multiple levels of narrowing: (1) Beauty as largely physical. (2) Physical appeal as largely sexual. What's next? How about defining sexual attraction in an especially narrow way?

While there are sexual attractions as diverse as the humans that experience them - sexuality has *also* increasingly come to be framed and presented in certain kinds of ways and packaging. In this crass commercialization of our culture, human bodies themselves have increasingly become a sexual commodity - turned into what writer and human rights activist Natasha Walter refers to as "living dolls."[24]

Taking it up a notch

These cultural demands are not lost on us. One woman said, "I feared that if men didn't notice my body right away, I would be invisible to them."[25] Referring to the high pressure on women "just to get noticed," one woman likened it to "a set of Darwinian social rules" demanding that women "dress and act a certain way to outperform other women competing for mates."[26]

While this kind of pressure is not new, 40% percent of women in a 2009 survey also said they felt more pressure to have the perfect body now than they did *just five years ago*.[27] "Expectations of physical beauty are so high" one woman said. "That's always been there, but it is different now."

When someone doesn't feel much interest from potential partners, it can become especially easy to adopt the mentality of "I have to stick out somehow!" The mindset, one woman explained, is "Gosh, I have to be really sexy, because nothing is really happening in this arena, so I've got to take it to the next level. I've got to really strut my stuff and show people what I've got." She concluded, "There is a real sense of desperation among women: 'what can I *possibly* do to get guys' attention?!'"

"There's this undercurrent of paranoia," one author writes - "that people are constantly watching and judging every inch of you, so you'd better be perfect."[28] One man said, "It's scary how it touches so much upon Hitler's ideas of the perfect race. There is an uncanny ring: you *have* to be beautiful to be worth something." One woman said: "Women look around, and see lots of competition or [maybe] my husband has problems with pornography, so I need to take it up a notch. What on earth is going on?"

Beauty impossible

That's my question too: What *on earth* is going on? More specifically, how many people can actually reach these standards of attractiveness in their lifetimes? In other words, how many people can actually become "beautiful"?

From within this cultural narrative, the answer, obviously, is *not everyone.*

In that same Harvard study, researchers found that "beautiful" is not a word most women even associate with themselves. Only two percent of women in the international study consider themselves "beautiful," even fewer than those choosing "cute" (7%), "good-looking" (7%) or "attractive" (9%). Data confirms that "women are less satisfied with their beauty than with almost every other dimension of life,"[29] with 90% of all women ages 15-64 worldwide wanting to "change at least one aspect of their physical appearance."[30]

Do you see the tension here? As summarized by the research team, "At the same time that women of all ages and classes want to claim beauty for themselves, there has been an *insidious narrowing* of the beauty aesthetic to a limited physical type...which inevitably excludes millions and millions of women." The very physical standards we have enshrined as highly desirable in our culture remain, they continue, "almost impossible to attain" and out of reach by most people, resulting in "considerable anguish" to otherwise healthy (and lovely) individuals.[31]

Relationships aborted

Make no mistake, this is not about knocking the idea of beauty or romance or chemistry or sexual attraction - not at all. All of those things can be precious, sweets part of love. The discussion here concerns the role sexual and physical attractions *should* play in our experience. And the notion we're considering here is this: It Should Be Everything.

Unsurprisingly, this story often "booby-traps relationships with an impossible expectation,"[32] resulting in relationships left in "shambles from the crushing burdens...placed on them."[33] Historian Coontz describes the common pattern - namely, that when a couple's romantic relationship "did not meet their heightened expectations, their discontent grew proportionately." The more people "hoped to achieve personal happiness [within intimate partnerships], the more critical they became of 'empty' or unsatisfying relationships."[34]

Whatever relationship in which we find ourselves, our minds can be focused on questions like: *Are you getting all you deserve from this relationship? Are you Feeling Enough? Is this person good enough?*

If our feelings don't meet the cultural standards, it then becomes easy to feel cheated or ripped off: *Is this the best I can do? Don't I deserve more?*

With questions like this floating around, any relationship (even good ones) become suspect. These same demands can also prevent relationships (including good ones) from ever getting started. One man admitted that in the past, "Unless I was completely blown away and infatuated, I had a hard time pursuing girls." The man who spoke of having to have his socks "knocked off" said, "This is how I'm going to feel when I meet the right woman. or this is how I want to feel," then added, "I passed up a lot of great girls since then because I wasn't *feeling that way.*"

One man said that he harbored "expectations that things work out perfectly and a tendency to terminate dating relationships because....maybe she doesn't fit 100% of the criteria I am looking for." One woman spoke of couples that "could have got married; they were perfect for each other and everyone is shocked. They are all well-suited, but one of the persons is always able to find something wrong."

In this way, relationships can remain burdened with "over-expectations concerning what the other person is Supposed To Be like." M. Blaine Smith writes of the common conviction "that you must not settle for anyone who less than fully measures up to your image of the ideal mate," an expectation that encourages individuals to be "quick to bail out of a relationship at the first sign of another's imperfections" or to "wait endlessly" for a perfect relationship to come along.[35] One person admitted, "Little things would kind of shake me and I wouldn't get to know a girl for this or that - physical imperfections."

This might be a good time to sit down and re-consider the story we've embraced and committed to - maybe taking a deep breath and re-thinking this a little?

We don't do this very often. Instead, what do we do? We do everything we can to *meet them,* working hard to find the experience we want. For current relationships, this can mean doing something, *anything,* that will finesse The Feeling to an acceptable point.

Keeping it exciting

You know what I'm talking about: "How to Make Your Man Happy," "Tips for Keeping the Excitement Alive in Your Relationship." The onus is on *you* to keep the fire going!

Have you ever seen a relationship struggling, and heard someone say, "Maybe you just need to get a little more physical. Maybe that will help the relationship?"

I found an opposite patterns in my own interviews. One man described a great connection with his girlfriend at the beginning; then he said, "Things went purely physical. All we would do is hang out, watch a movie and kiss - there wasn't much conversation and it fizzled in two weeks. It just died."

Another told me about this pattern in his relationships, "I would get really excited, kiss them, things would go well, then the bottom would fall out; all my feelings were gone, and I was just left with a desire to get out." Another told me:

It's really weird. When my girlfriend and I started dating, we would talk a lot and late into the night. We were together every single night and hung out a lot. But then things progressed to center on the physical. We started into making out and being passionate; we would talk less; they became surface-level conversations, and everything was physical. My feeling started to tank. Our relationship went from being together every single night till late, to not really wanting anything. This ruined a couple of my relationships.

Counter-intuitive effects of certain kinds of physical intimacy are currently being studied by several different research teams. Scientists at the University of Texas at Austin and UCLA, for instance, found that first sexual intercourse led a man to perceive "diminished attractiveness in a woman," especially if that person had several previous sexual partners. Reflecting on these findings, one commentator concludes, "Sex simply doesn't lead to love for men. And if the guy is a player, it more often leads to outright disdain."[36]

Scientists call this general pattern "hedonic adaptation." It's the same thing that happens with the fading thrill of a new job, a new home, a new outfit, etc. As summarized by Dr. Sonja Lyubomirsky, professor in the Department of Psychology at the University of California:

> We're inclined, psychologically and physiologically - to take positive experiences for granted. As if propelled by autonomic forces, our expectations change, multiply or expand and, as they do, we begin to take the new, improved circumstances for granted.[37]

This kind of adaptation is common with sexual passion and arousal. Laboratory studies from Melbourne, Australia, to Stony Brook, New York, have shown the same thing: arousal decreases and indifference grows as sexual experience is repeated.[38] As Raymond Chandler summarized: "The first kiss is magic. The second is intimate. The third is routine."

And that's no joke! As came up in my own interviews, depending on the circumstances, passionate kissing can have a counterintuitive effect on the progression of a relationship.

To be clear, the question we're considering here is not when to engage in sex or sexual kissing. The issue is why we feel we *have* to push the physical in the first place (especially before or beyond the place we are comfortable)?

And the answer I'm proposing is that our expectations of romance often seem to *demand it*. As relationships are required to measure up to "greater depths of emotional and physical intimacy than had been possible (or necessary) in the past,"[39] we thus come to experience "unanticipated and revolutionary consequences."[40]

Are there other consequences to this love story? It's time to buckle up. Because once we've embraced this view of romance, we're in for a ride.

Chapter 3. Driven: Romance Compelled

"When we fall out of love the world suddenly seems dismal and empty, even though we are still with the same human being who had inspired such rapture before." - Robert Johnson

She moved into town our 8th grade year, right smack dab in the middle of junior-high awkwardness. The first time I met her, she had braces, plaid clothes, and wore her backpack with both straps. In no time, she had captured my boyish heart.

For the next three years of school, she was the only girl in the world. I couldn't stop thinking about her, even making notes of what I would say to her between our phone calls. In the best and purest sense of young romance, I was smitten.

After sophomore Christmas dance, Junior Prom and numerous dates in between, we became a couple our senior year.

Then it happened...the unthinkable: my feelings changed. After years of dreaming and dating, I did the only thing that now made sense. I stopped calling.

The memory has never entirely lost its sting.

At the time, though, I truly saw no other way. This was just The Way I Was Feeling - with nothing much I could do about it.

Then it happened with another girl. And another. And I started hearing the same story from others - many times.

Across all this heartbreak, one of the striking and stand-out themes is the underlying sense of being *driven* in our experiences of love. Laying aside the positive sense of the word "driven," dictionary definitions also emphasize some kind of "outward force or current that compels someone to act in a particular way or move in a specific direction." The result of being "driven," then, is something that has happened forcibly - carried along and controlled by a certain compulsive need or coercive power.

And that's pretty much how it happens, right? We're driven towards someone by passion and driven away by a fade in passion. Relationship after relationship starts with a blaze of sweetness and excitement. We celebrate finding 'the one' we've been looking for, and enjoy the rush of our early time together.

Then, something changes. Feelings settle, then shift, then dissipate...leaving us adrift and with only one sensible option.

As one man put it, "abandon ship at all costs." "When...I lost those feelings and it made me nervous - in a way, I sabotaged it," another guy told me. "Once that died down," he explained, his excitement about being with his sweetheart was not there any-where: "I didn't *have anything to stand on.*"

And that quickly, the dream passes. "So long as we are 'in love' with someone," Robert Johnson writes, "the world takes on a brightness and meaningfulness." But when we fall out of love, he continues, everything changes, "The world suddenly seems dismal and empty," even though the same person who thrilled us is still available to us.[1]

Driven. Compelled. Why is this happening?

Just The Way Love Is

That's not the question I was asking myself. Instead of sitting down and thinking seriously about these things, it was easier to do something else: conclude that this was just how romantic love was!

I'm not alone. Most people I know have also taken for granted a view of love that is largely random, irrational and outside of our control. "One does not 'do' it, one does not control it, one does not understand it: It just happens," one author notes.[2] Another adds, "No matter how open to or eager for it we may be, the experience may still elude us."[3]

Feelings of love are expected to surprise us in their "intensity and suddenness,"[4] rising "ab nihilo - out of nothingness."[5] "You cannot learn to love" another writes, instead, love will "strike" in its own time and "you have no inkling when that time is."[6] Such love "comes quickly and flies away the same" writes Voltaire. "Like lightning it begins and ends in the same moment" adds Cervantes.

Love thus becomes a "spontaneous personal experience" derived from an impromptu "emotional reaction, of suddenly being gripped by an irresistible feeling,"[7] - "something one 'falls into' if one is lucky."[8]

As detailed earlier, we expect this feeling to be overwhelming and out of this world - a passion of dramatic proportions. In this sense, one author writes that love can become experienced as "an irresistible force, like gravity...like falling off a cliff, if you fall in love, nothing can be done about it....lovers are held in the grip of something larger than themselves and beyond their control."[9]

Consequently, this kind of love may spring up between strangers or after seeing someone in passing. And just as easily, just as fast, this "bewitchment and sweet tyranny of love" can reverse, "disappear[ing] in a moment, just as quickly and unexpectedly as it came."[10] And when it does, love's departure is experienced as largely outside of our control, as one woman reflected: "I'm just not interested as much as I thought I was. It's not in my control that I don't like you, but I *just can't feel it anymore*."

Beware the effort

Rather than seriously question our experiences of driven-love, then, we go on to embrace a view of romantic love that says it's driven by its very nature! It was Ben Franklin who proposed that by definition, "love is changeable, transient, and accidental." This lack of control has subsequently been celebrated as a welcome part of true love itself. As Erich Fromm put it, "Falling in love always verges on the abnormal; it is always accompanied by blindness to reality, and compulsiveness."[11]

The cultural commitment to this view of love is strong enough that any effort needed in a relationship can be seen with suspicion - as a kind of automatic sign that something may not be quite right. Referring to challenges that came up in a relationship, one individual said, "Just the fact that we have to talk about this is a sign that we shouldn't be dating."

Did you catch that? At any stage of a relationship, if you have to work at something as a couple, that Should Be raising some red flags for you (so the story goes). "Any attempt to introduce an element of choice" into a relationship, another author writes, "is seen as decidedly *un*romantic." One woman recollected telling herself during her engagement, "it shouldn't be this hard...true love *should be* easy."

Consequently, one sign of a relationship worth pursuing is if there is *little need for effort*. More than one possible element of love, this effortlessness can be seen as one of its defining qualities: "love is *best* when it is accidental and unintended."[12]

The romance we seek is thus "something that must happen by itself - without a conscious decision."[13] And so we wait for that feeling to distill upon us - waiting and hoping.

Just add water

Where energy and effort *are needed* in a romantic relationship, it is assumed that be very little. "Love thus becomes an action that is, by all accounts, fairly simple and straightforward - something "easily indulged in by anyone [with] nothing easier."[14] This kind of love, another author notes, demands "nothing more than the skills of an average, moderately experienced consumer."[15]

From within this story, then, when it comes to seeking love, it doesn't really matter how we live. Someone who is lazy and undisciplined is just as likely to find this love as an energetic and dedicated one. Falling in love, from this perspective, has little or nothing to do with our own internal development as persons.[16]

In this way, love relations come to mimic the same patterns of "exchange which govern the commodity and the labor market." One author elaborates, "In a consumer culture like ours, which favors products ready for instant use, quick fixes, instantaneous satisfaction, results [with] no protracted effort, foolproof recipes, all-risk insurance and money-back guarantees," the "love experience [is made] in the likeness of other commodities, that....promise to take the waiting out of wanting, sweat out of effort and effort out of results."[17]

Ease, effortlessness, irrationality, compulsiveness, accidentalness - if these are the defining indicators of love, no wonder that so many of us feel helpless in our romantic relationships.

Unthinkable

As mentioned earlier, when I walked away from my high school sweetheart, I saw little or nothing I could do about my changed feelings. It was simply, "sorry, I can't do this." You bet - I felt sorry for the pain it caused. But no matter how bad I felt, I simply could not see at the time what was happening.

The philosopher Gramsci argues that when a discourse or way of thinking is powerful enough, it renders anything outside its prescribed conditions invisible and "unthinkable."[18] That describes my experience well: once I lost The Feeling in a relationship, there was simply no possibility of being with that person any more; it was unthinkable.

If there was another way, a better way, it didn't matter. Because it wasn't even a possibility, wasn't even thinkable, in my world at the time. Instead, my relationships were shaped, guided (and punished) by the story outlined in previous chapters.

To review: When The Feeling is there - we follow. When it goes away - we retreat. If we feel a certain way, then we *are* a certain way: Feeling excited? I'm in love. Not feeling as excited? Not sure I'm in love anymore.

One man spoke about "waiting for a feeling to occur or appear" - a feeling that was so intense that he would not be interested in any other girl. He went on to explain that he would walk away from a relationship if he didn't have a "deep connection and want to be with her all the time." He added, that this is what "I've heard from people who've been in love, that that's what they feel, [therefore,] if I'm not feeling it, I'm not feeling it."

The consequences can be almost algorithmic in their application. If we're feeling it, we stick with it. If we're not feeling it, we conclude there's no way to move forward. Time to break up! Passively, albeit hopefully, we await our orders.

Sometimes you may even feel disappointed that your feelings have subsided because you thought you were really liking this one. Guess not, though, because The Feeling never lies, right?

Whatever the details, concluding "I'm in love" or "I'm not feeling it" can thus exert remarkable influence - raising a kind of moral imperative on the right steps to be taken in relationship. In these cases, a kind of ethical mandate arises: <u>Do not proceed without *feeling it*.</u>

Whether coming or going, the possession of romantic feeling becomes the deal-breaker and the single ingredient that we need for a relationship - "the one thing it cannot do without."[19] Without it, we have "nothing else to stand on." Once these feelings "evaporate," we take for granted that "there will be no more basis for a relationship."[20]

Once we equate love and strong passion, one researcher concludes, it has tangible, concrete effects on relationships. In particular, if that passion is not there, it's easy to assume one does not really love one's partner. Maybe then, the relationship should end?[21]

This applies to married couples as well, where the standards have "gradually shifted" one writer notes, "from one which required couples to remain married even if they were not in love to one which virtually demanded divorce unless they remained in love."[22]

Accordingly, we invoke love (or its lack) to justify otherwise painful choices. One historian explains, "Dissatisfaction leads individuals, in Schopenhauer's words 'to undertake every peril and conflict.' For its sake, men and women will impulsively discard everything else they value: honor, goods; family; friends; the achievements of a lifetime."[23]

No matter how good or full of potential a relationship may be, the drumbeat message continues: 'you deserve to feel more than this.' Or, 'it's not fair that you're stuck here.'

If a couple decides to re-commit to enriching their relationship, the rhetoric may turn more aggressive: 'Are you crazy? You don't feel enough...you *can't* go to this party...you *can't* continue to be with her.'

Resisting such feelings becomes seen as unhealthy and even pathological - an issue of honesty and identity - 'you need to be true to these feelings. In this way, we can fall into a kind of obedience and slavish commitment to The Feeling (or the lack therof) - e.g., 'if you're feeling something, you've gotta let yourself follow it!'

In this way, romantic passion quickly "seizes us against our will," another author notes, "stands us on our heads, turns our lives upside down, rearranges our loyalties." He continues, "We forget our precious plans, give up our beliefs, and abandon the ways of life to which we have clung."[24] This kind of emotional experience, one author notes, often "overrides reason, logic, good judgment and outside counsel and becomes the final authority for decision making."[25]

As a result, we come to accept powerlessness and lack of freedom in one of the most important decisions of life.

This naturally raises serious questions. For one, if love really is "uncontrollable" one researcher asks, "how can any individual be expected to approach a love relationship with maturity and responsibility?"

Good question! Pretty hard to ask *anything* from someone who has embraced this way of thinking. This same researcher concludes that "such individuals will be victims of fate and unable to take control of their lives, with all kinds of negative consequences for those who love them."[26]

Can you relate to any of this discussion about drivenness? Have you ever felt almost forced to do something like walk away in a relationship that you otherwise really valued? How aware were you of what you were doing at the time? Would a bigger awareness at that time about the influence of different cultural ideas have made any difference for you and that relationship?

In fairness, emotions are powerful. When we feel something, it's hard to not experience it as undeniable Reality. How exactly to relate to feeling and emotion in a way that we are not strangled and driven by them is a fascinating question taken up later in the book.

Running throughout this story, however, is one unquestioned assertion: *that what we're feeling is a reliable and accurate reflection both of Reality and of who we really are.*

Is that true? A very different story of love pivots around a very different answer to that precise question. For now, we conclude this discussion illustrating two of the more painful aspects of romantic drivenness: walking away from Mr./Miss Right and embracing Mr./Miss False Positive.

Walking away from great matches

Over the years of interviewing, I've met many people who have the same story as one man who described his pursuit of romance and said, "I passed up a lot of great girls since then because I wasn't feeling that way."

Notice that it doesn't matter whether that girl was a Good Match - his eye was on something else. If a simple, calm relationship offers us happiness, one author notes, "we won't accept it [because] it's 'too simple,' 'too dull.' We are trained to respect only what is inflated, hyper-intense, high-pressured, big and complicated." In this way, we often reject "ordinary humanness" as "too earthbound, too dull and sordid for our romantic prejudices."[27]

Consequently, we may condemn otherwise positive relationships as simply Not Enough, even when some level of real attraction and romantic feeling exists. If dramatic attraction is the goal, then less dramatic feelings may simply not measure up - similar to the man who told me that "Unless I was completely blown away and infatuated, I had a hard time pursuing girls."

As we live out of these storylines, we are stopping relationships from happening before they even have an opportunity to develop! Two people who would otherwise be attracted on a subtle, deeper level may thus simply overlook each other.

One woman suggested, "We're so focused on waiting for this big huge thing [with relationships], that we miss it. We don't ever see all the people walking by us every day that could be someone we could be with." "[Some] make it so profound and complicated," she said, "like 'well, I don't [know] yet' because it has to be some big huge thing." She continued, "We are looking for an over-whelming feeling, but it isn't like that. Life just happens; it isn't some big thing." In this way, she suggested, "we miss opportunities - don't recognize opportunities or possibilities we've been given."

I would know. Each time I walked away from someone, I was focused on the opportunity ahead and not the one I was leaving behind. At the time, of course, my reasons for walking away were varied: "Timing is not right...I'm just not in a good place...We're just not a good fit...it just hasn't worked out." "Powerful desire," one author notes, "never fails to explain itself."[28]

It's important to acknowledge that relationships sometimes end because they *should* end, for a variety of reasons. The message here is not that relationships should never end - it's that many relationships with amazing potential are ending prematurely: being aborted when maybe they really deserve to live!

But we don't see that. We *can't* see the unthinkable. Instead, we walk away, convinced that we'll find someone better - 'I just haven't met him yet; she's out there somewhere.' Lurching after The Feeling, we follow wherever it leads...even to places we don't really want to end up going after all.

Embracing Mr. (or Miss) Wrong

The same dynamics that lead individuals to *not embrace* those who are good for them can obviously work in the reverse direction - leading them towards someone who may or may not be the best match. One person went so far as to argue that the current culture around romance represents "the perfect methodology to ensure two perfectly incompatible people make themselves believe they're a match."[29]

Once physically involved with the wrong person, emotional bonds can develop. This is especially true, one author notes, for women, who are "wired to bond" and have a "pesky hormone" called oxytocin that can bind their hearts to a toxic companion.[30] Once 'under the influence' of these chemicals of hyper-intense romance, "we are as likely to fall in love with someone with whom we are obviously ill matched as with someone more suitable."[31]

Equally painful can be having to walk away from someone you have fallen for - then realized is wrong for you. Years after breaking up with Miss Right, I fell deeply in love with someone else. She was a wonderful, beautiful person that I came to adore easily. But as I fell more head over heels every day, a surprising dissonance and unmistakable lack of peace came over me. No matter what happened, I couldn't shake this feeling of wrongness about the relationship. Locked in by my feelings, I found myself in an impossible place - bound and drawn to her by intense passion, but also experiencing undeniable discomfort and unable to find any peace about continuing on. That moment and decision were the hardest and most painful of my life.

Are you seeing madness here? On one hand, we may be driven to love a poor match, with all the punishment that entails. But when paired with the right person, on the other hand, we do not feel enough of *something* to be satisfied. In both directions, we can feel literally constrained from choosing and doing what our core really needs: "we may not even like or admire the object of our passion, yet, try as we might, we may not be able to fall in love with a person whom we deeply respect and with whom a deep relationship would be in all ways desirable."[32]

Everywhere we turn, we're pushed and pulled and driven to this person and away from that one. We give our hearts away and take them back at the whim of a feeling.

Through all the torture, we rarely question - let alone notice - the subtle storyline running through our experience.

And that's the point of this book. Noticing. Expanding the discussion. Paying attention to the impact of a story that says *'if you want to have true love, make sure you're feeling constant, crazy-intense romance!!'*

Maybe it's time to stop obeying The Feeling. To pause, think, and watch. And think again.

Chapter 4. Tentative:
Romance Undecided

*"Relationships vacillate between a sweet dream and a nightmare,
and there is no telling when one turns into the other"*
- Zygmunt Bauman

It's hard when romantic relationships end. And it's hard when they
never start. But you want to know what's even harder? That mushy
middle-ground place far removed from any solid decisions, where
romantic relationships mostly start, sort-of continue and almost
end...every week or so: on again-off again, hot-and-cold, but still
together...mostly.

Once our eyes are fixed on hyper-intense romance, we've just
seen how changing feelings can take us for a relationship ride,
with our future fluctuating on the waves of vacillating emotion. So,
what's it like to date someone like that?

Will you still love me tomorrow?

"It was always the same thing" one woman said. "For the first two
months, the guy was *so* excited - *all* into it even sometimes to the
point of 'we're getting married.' As he gets excited and things are
so great, I give the relationship more as well." She continued, "As I
like him more, however, he starts to back off. The initial excitement wears off, and he finds things wrong with me."

A man described how it always seemed to get to the point
where his girlfriend wanted to get serious, but said, "I just wasn't
sure. I had a hard time feeling that was the right thing to do, with
stressful months trying to decide whether that's what I wanted." He
continued, "Eventually, it would end when she would get tired of
waiting or I would say that I couldn't do it."

This same man described many other friends who have been
"touch and go" right up until the marriage date. A woman recounted multiple experiences with men "who suffer when there is any

sort of pressure - resulting in a fine-line waiting game." She said, "I can't get away from that," reflecting:

> My sister just married a boy who absolutely adores her and would have waited 10 years for her. But in the men I date, there is some fear - or something in them that I don't understand - that they can't get over, like a cancer. The man I was supposed to marry, he just couldn't do it. He loved me and would have given me the world, but he just could not do it. I don't know what it is. I don't know and understand fully.

She continued:

> I sit here with my current boyfriend. He loves me and would give me the world - telling me, "I have no reason not to marry you." But he just can't do it. There is this anxiety that has to change and I don't know how to change it. I've heard that so many times: "I love you, and have no reason not to [move forward] - but I just have to get over this feeling."

Among the most maddening aspects of modern American romance is the level of ultra-tentativeness that has become almost a cultural norm. What's behind this "chronic state of romantic irresolution"?[1] Is this just something we all need to get used to? Or is this perhaps something we should *not* get used to - something we should investigate and autopsy, until we really figure out what is crippling and killing good relationships?

Let's do it. But breathe deep...because like most autopsies, it's not pretty! If you ever feel faint of heart or discouraged, keep reading. It gets better!

Missing something?

Things have been awesome for awhile. Sweet. Fun. Exciting.

Then it hits: a heat-sinking missile of a question that goes something like this: "yes - he's really great. Super guy - but...aren't we Missing Something here?' One man said the following experience happened over and over: "[I] go out with a girl four times and I'm interested...but then for whatever reason, I think, 'this relationship is lacking; this doesn't have what I'm looking for' - not that something is wrong with you or me, but we're *missing something*. Something is lacking."

And of course, in many cases, something important *is* lacking. As mentioned earlier, there are 100 really good reasons to end a relationship - all of which are worth considering.

There are just as many reasons to end a relationship that are really pathetic, however. A woman described a relationships where "for the first two months, he was so excited and all into it to the point of 'we're getting married' - wondering when he was going to get to meet my parents...things were so great." "But as I liked him more," she continued, "he started to back off." The initial excite ment wore off, she explained, "as he found things wrong with me. My voice was not sweet enough and sometimes he thought I chewed too loud. I knew things were bugging him...so I worked trying to fix all the little things." When he asked for time to 'figure it out,' this man said to her, "80% is really good, but the other 20% [less so]...I really like some things about you and I am trying to decide if I can deal with the other things."

Once again, some of that 20% could be sticking points that deserve to stick! In other cases, it's hard to tell whether small things should be hijacking a relationship. A man described one small characteristic of his girlfriend turning into something big that bothered and "ate" at him.

Sometimes we worry things are missing - other times we're worried about things that are already there - that we wish were not. Whether absent or present, big or small, these worries can hit even couples with the hugest, greatest compatibility and potential. In that moment, how easy it can be to say something like, "I like you, but I just don't know if it's enough."

If not one question, then another is sure to arise.

But is it right?

Whether or not individuals move forward often depends on whether they *feel right* about the relationship. One man said "every girl I dated was terrific, it was just a question of *whether we were right for each other.*" This can mean various things. For some, rightness implies some kind of divine approval - for others, it may reflect an overall sense of whether a person is a good enough fit or match. Still others may equate 'it's right' with whether 'I feel enough' for this person - or a decision of whether they feel personally ready, or whether this is the right time.

Careful evaluation on any of these points is surely a good thing. In some cases, however, we can overdo it - thinking too much about whether something is right or not. Indeed, the fear of making a bad choice can paralyze individuals searching for a spouse - as one person described it, "They are terrified of making a mistake...They think too much and overanalyze everything."[2] One man described a previous engagement where things were going well and he was "really excited." But after a period of smooth sailing, he started asking, "Do I really want this?" He continued:

> That's where I started to overanalyze and think about every-thing she did and whether I liked it or not - all her attributes and what I knew about her. That was the point where...my feelings went from being relaxed and just enjoying her and being excited - to stress, overanalyzing and...even though she was the same person, not feeling the same way I did before.

He finished the story, "She could sense things were different. I just didn't have the courage to end things; I wanted to keep trying. I remembered what I felt before and wanted to get back to that, but I didn't know how. Eventually she got frustrated and said she couldn't handle it anymore, basically."

Sound familiar to anyone? Keep trying, and trying some more - anything to summon The Feeling again...Maybe it's not the right time?...Can I take this anymore?

At some point, it all becomes too exhausting, and easier to simply keep searching and checking out other options. After all, one man said, "when the timing is right and I've met the right person, I have no doubt it will happen."[3]

Someone better?

And then it happens! We meet someone great - and nothing seems to be missing. It *feels right*, and things are headed in the *right direction*.

Despite wonderful signs, though, another fear creeps in: this may be good...but is it *the best?*

- One man said, "There's always going to be another woman that will be more attractive, intriguing, a mystery."
- Another man admitted, "My biggest problem is that I'm always looking for the next big thing...I never really stick with one girl, or give that girl a fair chance."
- Another said "part of my problem was always thinking something better would come along" - admitting, "it's hard to accept someone imperfect with this in mind."
- Another guy acknowledged, "It is really hard to not ask yourself if you are going to 'miss out' on other opportunities if you decide to date one girl."

Can you relate with any of these comments? Have you ever been romantically involved with someone pretty amazing - but felt unable to totally commit yourself to that person for some of these same reasons? How did you respond and handle it? What do you think the answer to these kinds of fears and concerns is? I'd love to hear your thoughts on these questions - and others explored in the book. If you're ever interested and willing to share some things directly, check out www.notfeelingit.org.

Whatever the details, fears of committing to the wrong person can be very real. One man said, "You don't want to be worried, am I going to get to the point that I'm not attracted to this person and have regrets at marrying them? That was a fear." Images of moving forward in a 'loveless match' can be conjured up - reflecting Jane Austen's famed caution that "anything is to be preferred or endured rather than marrying without affection."[4]

And to be fair, it's true that in any given case there definitely could be someone better out there for you. The issue here is when we become fixated on the question - perpetually "chasing [our] projection of perfection, with the 'perfect [person]' always elusive on the horizon."[5] An obsession with finding the perfect match seems especially prevalent in places with an abundance of high caliber people, producing a kind of "market mentality" as individuals think, "I am dating a 9.7, but if I wait, maybe I could get a 9.9."[6]

One author spoke bluntly that expectations in both genders are "out of whack": "Every guy thinks he deserves a model. Every woman thinks she deserves a rich guy (who looks like a model)....They're convinced they're holding out for what they *deserve* - and what they deserve is the top 1 percent of the dating population. (Their parents told them they're awesome, and they believe it!)"[7]

Unchecked, this kind of astronomical ideal can become a breeding ground for inevitable discontent and endless searching. Like a moving target, our ideal keeps just ahead of us - eluding us like the shadow we used to chase as a child.

Shopping for a human being

As one person is abandoned for another who seems more exciting, relationships come and go in passionate, brief spurts - propelled towards and away from someone, at times, simply by an appetite for something new. One man said, "I think a lot of people get bored being with one person. They will enjoy being with one girl, then they get tired of them, and say, 'time to move on to the next one.'" Like television shows or ice cream flavors, relationships become something we enjoy for awhile, before we get 'bored' or 'tired' of the taste.

"We become consumers in a quest for the perfect product," one author noted, "forever upgrading to the new and improved model" and "never quite content with what we have because we see so many others out there that might be better but are *just slightly out of reach* or beyond our budget."[8]

This grueling shopping effort makes any given relationship difficult to sustain. To enjoy one person alone can become a baffling struggle, especially in an era of internet dating, as we can literally "always have another person on the line." The possibilities, one woman recollected, seemed "tantalizingly endless - even if they aren't." She said, "I always assumed there would be another setup, another guy at a party, or another online prospect."[9]

In otherwise positive relationships, the curiosity about 'someone better,' can drive couples towards unnecessary silliness. One woman described a man telling her he wanted to keep dating her - but asking to "ask other girls out, just to be sure" - showing her a paper in his wallet he used to evaluate all his dates. Another woman said:

> You know it's over when the person says (pick one): (a) "This week is going to be terrible. I'm completely swamped." (b) "I think maybe we should cool things for a while." (c) "A little voice tells me something isn't right." (d) "I've been doing a lot of thinking lately."[10]

Better. More. Not Enough. Missing Something. Is it any wonder that so many of us are walking away? Based on these conclusions, that's the only logical thing *to do!*

Breaking up isn't hard to do

Maybe it shouldn't be surprising then, that experts conclude individuals are currently walking away from committed relationships more casually than ever before and "at lower thresholds of unhappiness now than in the past."[11] In the case of married couples, for instance, only 15% of respondents in one national survey believed that a married couple with children should stay together "even if they don't get along."[12] The meaning of "not getting along," according to another study, "is being defined down," with estimates that more than half of recent divorces occur not because of high conflict, but because of "softer forms of psychological distress and unhappiness."[13] Political scientist Andrew Hacker argues that men and women are both less willing to make the concessions and take on the obligations that make a relationship last.[14]

More than simply an issue of willpower, past trauma can complicate issues of trust and love. One man who grew up in a divorced family, for instance, said the experience "fundamentally changes something about your belief that other people will be there for you, and that things can last, and that things will be permanent." He added, "the commitment to work it out with the person they are with seems to be diminished. The easier way is just to get out of the relationship."

Another child of divorce spoke of the "ultra care" he was taking in making decisions about relationships. He said, "If you get hurt enough in a family, you don't want to trust. I don't trust people. I lived in a family of yelling every day, [around] 'shut-ups' and anger all the time." He detailed the impact of this experience on his struggle to feel safe in relationships and know how to love.

For this and other reasons, enduring, exclusive and steady commitment has increasingly become a rare and endangered species.

Checking out our options

So what do we do instead? When challenges arise in a relationship, we've been trained in this larger story to do the obvious: check out our other options.

In this era where online dating has become mainstream, it's common to hear suggestions that internet dating merely replicates older trends, such as mail-order brides or personal ads.

I disagree. We've never seen anything like this: endless streams of polished images paraded before us, any time of day or night. This astronomically larger mating market has never existed before - with consequences we're only now realizing. As one writer concludes, the internet is "likely to be as influential in shaping the patterns of mating in the early 21st century as the internal combustion engine was in shaping the patterns of youthful dating in the early 20th century."[15]

For starters, the sheer number of other options alone can begin to jam the decision making process. When asked to choose one option out of many desirable choices (e.g., like shoes in a shoe store), researcher Barry Schwartz has found that individuals begin to focus on missed opportunities rather than the potential right in front of them.[16]

And with a seemingly endless array of options - each looking just a bit better - can you blame them? Real life behavior can begin to mimic the pornographic culture in a subtle way, with an even more enticing option always available on just the next page.

"Whoever you are dating or married to" one man said, "I can always pick out a picture of someone to show you that is more physically attractive."

If that is the case, how can someone ever commit to a lasting relationship? Call it the George Clooney effect. Call it the predictable consequences of a narrow narrative of love. Whatever we call it, the problem is pretty clear: astronomical expectations and a storyline that inevitably breaks down in real life. As one man admitted: "I had this idea that I could and would be able to get a girl who was essentially physically perfect for me. She would satisfy my physical needs in a perfect manner."

No wonder we're stuck! (Heaven have mercy on this man's future spouse!)

Crippling fear

And this is the tragedy: When surrounded by all the options, we simply don't recognize when beauty arises right in front of our eyes. This was my story - and maybe it's yours. Always waiting for the next set-up around the corner, the party where that person will be there: 'Don't worry...she's out there!...Just wait longer, and you will find someone *amazing*.'

When I did meet someone, I became so engrossed in making sure I felt enough about her that I hardly saw the person in front of me. In this way, truly lovely individuals may be abandoned in our search for 'someone better.' That obsession with finding "the right person," can lead you to fail to see the good in people you are with, one man said, since "there will always be someone better." He concluded, "You can't keep looking for it forever."

Or maybe you can? If expectations are high enough, a life-long search doesn't seem out of the question. After all, we're searching for the most amazingly attractive person we've have ever met - or *will* meet - someone to provide us endless passion.

And indeed, once this is the goal, it's hard to imagine how any relationship could survive. As one man admitted, "When I was attracted to someone, there were still other girls on the radar. I would see another girl walk by, 'wow, she's prettier than the girl I'm with. I wonder what she's like.'" This man concluded "If I'm still attracted to other girls in my head, maybe I'm not ready to commit to this other girl?'" Another man who struggled for a long time being able to commit, admitted that he couldn't bear the idea that he may see girls after marriage that were more attractive than his wife.

Men aren't the only ones with such fears. Historian Stephanie Coontz describes a time in the 19th century when many women went through "marriage trauma," worrying about what would happen if a spouse did not live up to their high ideals. She describes two famous women of the time as having "recurrent nightmares about marrying unworthy men (neither ever married)."[17]

Such fears are alive and well today, thanks to the various forms of what contemplative traditions might call "mind-weather": 'She's not pretty enough for you...Can you see yourself being excited about her?...I don't think so.' or 'You are good enough looking that you deserve better than *this*...keep moving.'

And we do. We keep moving. Fearing - and moving on.

Commitment as restriction

At this point, the thought of sticking with one person starts to feel stifling and scary. If the relationship in question doesn't have Enough Feeling, Enough attraction, Enough beauty, Enough fulfillment, why would we stay? If there is a possibility of finding More Feeling, More attraction, More beauty, More fulfillment in someone else, then why in the world would we want to commit to this person?

From this vantage point, commitment becomes a risky and perilous thing, threatening to keep us from the very thing we most want. The very idea of "relationship" in current society, Zygmunt Bauman writes in his book *Liquid Love*, "tells of the pleasures of togetherness in one breath with the horrors of enclosure [...] In lasting commitments," he continues, "[we] spy out oppression; in durable engagement, [we] see incapacitating dependency":

Investing your feelings into the current relationship is always a risky step. Investing strong feelings in your partnership and taking an oath of allegiance means taking an enormous risk: it makes you dependent on your partner...The advice is 'don't let yourself be caught. Avoid embraces that are too tight. Remember, the deeper and denser your attachments, commitments, engagement, the greater your risk.[18]

The idea is this: "When committing yourself, remember that you are likely to be closing the door to other romantic possibilities which may be more satisfying and fulfilling - surrendering the right to 'hunting out pastures new.' If you want fulfillment, do not make or demand commitments. Keep all doors open at any time." On a number of levels, this larger narrative of romance incubates a fear of cutting oneself off from all other options. By maintaining only casual commitments, individuals thus "leave the door wide open to 'other romantic possibilities' that...may 'be more satisfying and fulfilling.'"[19]

In this way, individuals may see total, exclusive commitment as effectively working against their own well-being and happiness - a "trap" that shuts down other options and should be "avoid[ed] more than any other danger."[20]

Speaking of his hesitations before marriage, one man said, "For me, it was the word 'forever.' I haven't done anything for more than two years. How am I going to do something forever?"

Keeping it loose

In light of these very-real fears, individuals may understandably come to decide that they "must always keep their options open, they must always reserve the right to follow wherever their attraction goes."[21]

According to award-winning Polish scholar Zygmunt Bauman, a survivor of the Holocaust, the central figure of our current epoch is "the man or woman with no bonds, and particularly with none of the fixed or durable bonds [...] The denizen of our liquid modern society" he writes, still relates to others, but does so "having no bonds that are unbreakable" - instead, entering into "loose and eminently revocable partnerships" that "must be tied loosely so that they can be untied again, quickly and as effortlessly as possible, like a light cloak that could be 'thrown aside at any moment.'"[22]

This "high turnover, low-commitment pattern"[23] mimicks the cold business-like mentality we use in developing our careers. As one man said, "It's like online job applications, you can target many people simultaneously. It's like darts on a dart board, eventually one will stick."[24]

One woman was asked out on a date for Friday night. "At 10 p.m., I hadn't heard from him," she said. Finally, at 10:30, he sent a text message: "Hey, I'm at Pub & Kitchen, want to meet up for a drink or whatever? I'm here with a bunch of friends from college."

This woman (who declined) - went on to describe her social life as centered around "a cycle of text messages, each one requiring the code-breaking skills of a cold war spy to interpret." These messages, she continued, are "one step below a date, and one step above a high-five."[25]

From "Is anything fun going on tonight?" to "Hey" or "'sup," another person writes, "I've seen men put more effort into finding a movie to watch on Netflix, than composing a coherent message to ask a woman out."[26]

In place of the courage, planning and investment required to ask someone on a date, these communications are "more like dropping a line in the water and hoping for a nibble."[27] These limitations are typically overlooked, however, as frequent electronic check-ins "make a pretend relationship feel real."[28]

The death of dating

While some may want relationships to feel real - that's the last thing others seem to want! One man spoke of men's sincere reluctance to take women "to the French restaurant, or buy them jewelry, because those steps tend to lead to 'eventually, we're going to get married.'[...]So it's a lot easier to meet people on an even playing field, in casual dating. The stakes are lower."[29]

This isn't simply a male preference. One man spoke of "10-15 instances of girls flaking out of previously agreed-upon dates via text at the last possible minute," admitting it was "*way* easier" to get a girl to show up to an informal hang out or to tag along to an event, when compared to a committed date: "I think there's a sense that girls feel a lot of pressure to immediately make a decision about how she feels about a guy on a date" another man reflected: "She doesn't have a graceful way out. She might have to reject him....It's a lot of pressure."[30]

In recent decades, dating culture has dramatically withered and died across most of the country - notably, where it used to thrive the most. A large study of college life conducted at Columbia University concluded that "traditional dating is largely dead on college campuses," with students across the country telling them, "There is no such thing as dating here."[31] Another author writes that "campus social life had ceased to be organized around couple dating," with this courtship system virtually disappearing and being declared "obsolete." This "upending of dating culture" has led some people to encourage an embrace of new norms within a "post-dating" landscape.[32]

And what might those be? According to teen movies and some television programs, the one option left is relationship anarchy - joining masses of singles engaging in a sexual free-for-all.

While this hook-up culture gets a lot of attention in the mass media, statistics show it's been hyped far beyond its pervasiveness. While 20% in one national survey reported sex on a first date and 40% have experienced a hook-up, majorities of singles still report an interest in holding off and reserving themselves on some level. With the hook-up culture being portrayed as pervasive, however, research has found that people are experiencing subtle pressure to just go for it.[33] "Even securely attached women" one author notes, are "participating in unwanted sex and performing sexual acts they feel uncomfortable with." She underscores, "Every night, 20 percent of men we don't know well - who wouldn't be trusted with the keys to our house to water our plants - are given access to our bloodstreams and our eggs on a first date."[34]

At some point, of course, partners may get the keys to the house too.

Won't you be my roommate?

For many years, our mating system centered around a stepped, progressive system of advancing commitment - moving from casual socializing or dating, to pairing off as a couple, to a mutual decision of marriage, to announcing that engagement publicly. This all culminated in a social celebration and wedding ceremony. As Barbara Whitehead summarizes, "Each step becomes progressively more public. Each level has greater institutional recognition and social support" - as a couple is shaped and supported towards a moment of expressing total commitment publicly.[35]

This established system has been turned on its head, however, with a very different system taking its place.[36] Rather than a stair-step ladder of progressing commitment, today's mating system encourages cutting right to the chase. Most people of all educational levels, Dr. Kay Hymowitz and colleagues write, "are entering their first coresidential relationship at about the same age as in the past; it's just that now they are far more likely to be living together than married."[37] Individuals who decide to live together may do so without formally proposing anything or committing to anything in totality. All a guy has to do, one author notes, is "spend a lot of time at her place, let his clothes, sports gear, and toiletries accumulate, and then wonder out loud whether it makes sense to pay two rents."[38]

The provisional, spontaneous nature of these "mutually consenting, but free to leave" relationships mean partners may harbor very different expectations: "People can slide into living together, without any serious discussion or mutual understanding as to its meaning, purpose, or likely duration, and without much preparation, other than renting the U-haul."[39]

While this lack of clarity may be precisely what people want - it can also cause problems. One author notes, "In cohabiting partnerships, a vast world of obscure meaning, consisting of incidents, gestures, and casual commitments, has to be deconstructed and interpreted with an eye to...future intentions." For instance, "What did he really mean when he said, *Let's make this anniversary really 'special'?* Could it mean a ring? In the fog, it is easy to misinterpret." This author goes on to recount the story of a woman telling her boyfriend when they moved in together, "Gee, if we keep this up, we might end up getting married." He responded "huh" - or it might have been an affirmative "uh-hun" - which she took it as a "yes." When he announced three years later that he wanted to see other women, she was devastated. The author writes, "While she had been thinking about brides-maids, he had been checking out the babes."[40]

"While it once was liberating for women to break all the rules," Dr. Wendy Walsh writes, "it has created an environment in which men no longer feel they need to use courtship to obtain sex" - what she calls a "high-supply sexual economy."[41] Barbara Whitehead elaborates: "In the past, men faced obstacles in per-suading a nice girl to have sex without making special efforts to romance her, to prove themselves worthy, and to earn her affec-tions. Today, single guys...can count on a pool of attractive peer women" who are basically willing to do "whatever the men want."[42] Walsh concludes, "When sex is in high supply, men are less likely to commit."[43]

It's a pretty good point. If you're getting everything you want, what's the point of making any higher commitment?

Whatever the reasons, many singles end up "squander[ing] precious years by settling for no-criteria or low-criteria relation-ships" that fulfill little of their dreams and leave them feeling worse when they are over.[44]

Love me or leave me alone

In a variety of ways, then, and on a number of levels, once we embrace the dominant story of romance, tentativeness rules the day. Relationships, as we started the chapter, thus often "vacillate between a sweet dream and a nightmare, and there is no telling when one turns into the other."[45]

Even when moving forward in a relationship, a low-level, "perpetual uncertainty" can linger on - reflected in "acute, deeply felt and troublesome incarnations of ambivalence" - with individu-als often "torn among the conflicting forces and loyalties that rage."[46]

Given this remarkable fragility, no wonder we monitor our level of romantic attraction continually, as if we were using a feeling thermometer: 'am I feeling it today? How much?' Even the slightest changes in "emotional undercurrents" are monitored -

looking out for "something that you did not bargain for" to prompt you to know it's time to move on.[47]

More often than not, however, after we "endure incredible drama" and chronic tension, the same result emerges: "the passion simply fades and/or migrates to another person."[48]

The ambivalence explored above can hit any of us - men or women. When it does, we can all come to resemble the cowboys in Pam Houston's novels - "wild and fearless" in so many other adventurous life activities, but when it comes to love, unable to "venture anything so brave or daring" as commitment to one person.[49]

Chapter 5. Sapped: Romance Depleted

"There are still a few men who love desperately."
- J.D. Salinger

There you have it. Once you've committed to the dominant storyline of romance, you might want to brace yourself for what's likely to play out in your relationship - including any of the following: chronic uncertainty, maddening drivenness, and the potential of being crushed like a bug under some astronomical expectations.

Living out these larger cultural scripts, otherwise amazing individuals in hopeful relationships can thus become deeply traumatized. For one woman, "horrible dates and broken hearts were as common as snowstorms in Colorado" - each year she experienced several.[1]

"With each betrayal and breakup" another individual writes, "the emotional costs mount" - leaving in its wake a "complicated stew of anger, regret and rue" alongside "relationship fatigue." The "residue of mistrust and hurt" left in its wake can make some "wary of future relationships" similar to plaque on teeth that "builds up, hardens, and is often tough to get rid of."[2]

As relationship pain becomes the norm, the mounting, recurring wounds can start to add up - ultimately knocking the air out of us, romantically speaking.

How exactly does that happen?

De-learning love

In recent decades, the body has surprised us. Research has discovered a surprising degree of changeability in both the brain and body - especially following different kinds of life experiences and traumas. The trauma of relationship heartbreak has a particular power to shape our emotional and physical tendencies - especially over time.

Some individuals can find themselves "sexually numb and emotionally shut-down" - not able to feel intimate with anyone.[3] As individuals pursue a string of "love-less mergers."[4] they can be led. in the words of one sexuality researcher. to "associate sexuality with ambivalence. boredom. isolation. and loneliness" - leading them go after and miss out on the romance, intimacy, and satisfying sex they deserve.[5]

Following a combination of painful love experiences, it's even possible to see a one's own capacity to love degrade over time. As "the string of intermittent, brief, love episodes grows longer" one observer suggests we may come to experience a literal "de-learning of love" to the point of experiencing a "trained incapacity" for loving.[6]

Our capacity to feel empathy and tenderness can thus become disabled in a fundamental way. One man spoke of a gradual process of "losing sensitivity" in his own life, which included his own affection "dulling" and "capacity for love diminishing." Another person spoke of dating people who are "very on the ball, but inside, they are kind of hollow," adding "It's just hard for them to make relationships with people." Another spoke of people who "seem to be doing everything needed, so solid, so good," yet baffling in being able to offer "so little in real love."

I was one of those baffling boys! And not because I was dumb, or not trying, or deficient in skills or technique. My heart was simply confused in the deepest possible way.

Just not interested

Has your heart ever felt confused? Different than a confused mind, I'm talking here about confusion at our core - in this case, in the basic way we relate to those around us.

That's where we are today as a society with romance, I believe. As quoted earlier, one author writes with concern of an "eroding individual appreciation of the unaltered human form."[7] "Everyone has access to the prettiest women there are. all the time" one man said, leading to an "inflated idea of average in what he perceives as pretty and what he feels is attractive." This change, he clarifies, "is not just a mistaken idea or a conscious shift, but a change in what one actually feels - even physiologically."

Rest assured, this is not just one dude's opinion! As mentioned in the introduction, a report issued by the American Psychological Association on the "sexualization of girls in America" states something that deserves to be repeated: *"Exposure to narrow ideals of female attractiveness may make it difficult for some men to find an 'acceptable' partner or to fully enjoy intimacy with a female partner."*[8]

One study cited in the same report notes that within the current media atmosphere, "many individuals have become uncomfortable with 'real bodies' given the pervasiveness of stereotypes." In turn, "participants who reported greater comfort with women's real bodies were significantly more likely to be involved in a committed relationship."[9] Based on interviews with over 100 girls, another researcher remarked that "from early on, children are growing up with a distorted sense of what a normal woman's body is," adding that "suddenly a normal woman's body looks abnormal."[10]

One counselor claimed that increasing numbers of his clients are "suffering from a syndrome [he] dubbed Sexual Attention Deficit Disorder." He continued, "Just as people with real ADHD tend to be easily distracted, guys with SADD have become so accustomed to the high levels of visual novelty and stimulation that they're unable to focus on a real woman."[11]

Among other things, "the onslaught of porn" Naomi Wolf argues, has been "deadening male libido in relation to real women" and leading men to see "fewer and fewer" women as attractive. She continues:

Far from having to fend off porn-crazed young men, young women are worrying that as mere flesh and blood, they can scarcely get, let alone hold, their attention."[12]

In this way, we find ourselves pursuing a smaller and smaller subset of people: "It seems as though 70-80% of the guys....are chasing only 10-20% of the girls" one man said - adding that any girl who isn't physically ideal is overlooked in a media atmosphere that has trained us to believe that what is attractive "is only the top tie." I heard a lot of this in the interviews:

- "I would always go for the girls who wouldn't give me a chance."
- "I had this idea that I could and would be able to get a girl who was essentially physically perfect for me."
- "If the girl is not smoking hot, they don't waste their time getting to know her. Physically, there is a very specific type, and if you are not that type, then [they] are very judgmental."
- "I waste way too much time going after girls that I really don't have a shot with."
- "I feel like I've got to date this really, really pretty girl, so I eliminate a lot of girls there."

In a vicious cyle, disappointment with not having the ideal can breed even more disapointment. Being troubled with the "impossibility of maintaining the original idealization" can lead, one researcher notes, to behaviors that cause even more problems (avoiding interaction, lack of emotional support towards one's partner, etc.) that make it hard to maintain a relationship.[13]

To the extreme, some come to experience disinterest in lasting relationships, period. Musician John Mayer recently commented that he had no need for a romantic partner in his life, given the endless options he could find through online porn. One man said, "There were only a handful of girls at any point that I was attracted to. I would meet a girl once a year that I could see myself dating, and I couldn't ever connect with them."

John Mayer is not alone. One man said, "I would get along with certain girls like two peas in a pod, but I would feel zero urge to keep the relationship going." While there are definitely shy people out there, another person wrote that lack of interest in normal people is more prevalent than a lack of social courage. In terms of pursuing a relationship, he continued, "the grass doesn't look any greener, and so we all just end up staying on our current lawn."[14] "I don't feel like there is someone that I am attracted to" another man said - "I feel like there are a lot of guys in the same boat: generally good guys who really want to [commit]...who don't know exactly where to look."

This used to be my experience as well. I remember being surrounded by hundreds of people my age in college and feeling little or no interest in dating any of them. It is this perceived lack of options, of course, that becomes the explanation for our lack of interest: "hey - there's just *nobody* here I want to date."

Have you ever felt like this - that there was "no one" you want to pursue in a community of thousands? Have you ever walked away from an amazing person - because he or she wasn't amazing enough? If you've felt apathy about relationships previously, have you seen that change over time? If so, how? Lastly, what's your current level of interest in dating and pursuing a relationship?

Thanks for letting me ask so many questions! Wherever you find yourself, we're starting to get some clarity about why many intimate relationships are struggling these days. To summarize, as individuals' capacity for attraction and love decreases and their disinterest and apathy grow, it's no surprise that actual relationships stall, dissolve, or never happen at all! This includes budding relationships between couples that could, otherwise, be wonderful matches.

Wounded

Of course, there *are* people to date - even if we're unable to see them. If we can't see them as viable possibilities, however, they become largely irrelevant. "Many of my friends just aren't getting asked out," one woman said. Another person described many friends "who have virtually no dating experiences; they will get asked out on a date every 5 years or so."

One woman reflected, "You want to be noticed. You want guys to want you - it is very demoralizing. One of my roommates has not been asked out for 2 year. It makes her cry when she talks about it. No one is willing to try and get to know her as a person." Another woman described guys "not even want[ing] to take a second look at [her] and denying [her] immediately." She asked, "Do you know what kind of hurt that is?" Another woman spoke of wrestling with the nagging idea that "you are not good enough to be chosen by a man." She described "standing against the wall at a dance, while the men walk up to you, eye you up and down, and move on."

Like the star-bellied and plain-bellied Sneeches in Dr. Seuss's book, a kind of class system ensues, with a large group of people separated out as undesirable. You are either attractive or you are not. Speaking of her roommate, one woman said, "You go out with her - say, to a party - and forget about it, because the guys just want to know about her." Another woman who could "count on one hand the times I've been asked out" described eventually getting asked out by someone who was indecisive and unsure of his feelings for her. She reflected, "I didn't assume I was any special beauty; I just assumed he was having a hard time making a decision because there could be a lot cuter girls he could fall for."

Ongoing experiences like this can be especially difficult to process, to say the least. One woman described most of her life experience being "dominated by my attractiveness (or lack there-of)." She explained, "I have typically lots of good guy friends...I have been told by a number of them that they really liked me, that they really thought I was the coolest girl, but they weren't 'attracted' to me.[...]That is an interesting thing to be confronted by," she continued, "particularly because they are good men - they are generous...treating people well, and not chauvinistic."

When I asked her, "How did you reconcile that?" she responded, "I don't think I did. I told myself lies; I cried a lot and got new guy friends. I started over and ran from the problem." The core question for her remained, "What does it mean to not be attractive to another person? What does it mean when a guy doesn't like me enough to ask me out?"

It's easy to start to wonder, "Is it me?" Another woman said "I must not be doing something right because somehow I'm *not enough*. It's really hard to believe that I'm enough." She continued, "I thought that my job was to be myself, and naturally someone would like me. That's what I thought - 'if I can be myself with a person that I like then they will like me back.' But that's not true," she concluded. "It still doesn't mean they choose you."

Waiting for Superman

All of this was invisible to me, of course. Because I was on a quest - and needed to keep my eye on the ball. Rather than question what is happening - it was much easier to take for granted, as Johnson writes, that "it is a wonderful thing to search for our ideal, rather than settle for the flesh-and-blood woman that real life has put into his arms." [15]

And that's just what I did - continuing to charge forward, seeing myself as doing my best and courageously seeking the Right Person. In our romantic fog," Johnson continues about this common path, "we think this is very noble, very 'liberated,' but in fact it is just a misunderstanding of reality." [16]

But wait a minute. Let's not give up quite yet on this theory of romance. It's a big old world, and theoretically, if we find someone 'beautiful enough,' we should be able to fall head over heels in love for good, right?

Has anyone ever tested this hypothesis experimentally?

Actually, yes, in several seasons. The research study commonly known as "The Bachelor(ette)" started with a bold hypothesis - they had discovered a method to unite happy couples for life-long romance.

It goes like this: One bachelor (or bachelorette) has dozens of available partners paraded before him or her. Each specimen looks like Greek gods or goddesses - wearing and displaying physical perfection that the rest of us can only crave.

Week by week, the selected individual carefully, systematically, and methodically culls through all these glorious options - talking with, sizing up, and taste-testing each person physically, all to help decide what he or she really, really...*really*, wants. Each week, the pool thins until the "best of best" remain. Then, the dream partner is picked.

What a remarkable method! Their success rates must be phenomenal, no?

In 24 combined seasons of the *Bachelor*'s and *Bachelorette*'s match-making dream, 2 couples have ended up together for good -

with the remaining 22 pairs (91%) "not working out" quite like they had hoped.

Good thing we're not trying to follow that method in our own lives, right?!

Running from real people

After walking away from lasting relationships over and over, it's hard not to ask the obvious: Is this what we're really seeking after all? Maybe there's something more (or less) than lasting relationships that we really want - something else even more important to us than the relationships we're abandoning?

Research suggests that individuals who cheat in relationships are seeking to experience the rush of new romance and physical involvement - as a way, it seems, of "prolonging indefinitely the early and intoxicating phase of infatuation in a relationship."[17] Could this be what we're after...that rush, that romance, that *feeling* - sometimes despite our long-term relationships?

If so, then it makes sense why all the merely human people around us simply hold only passing interest for us. The larger culture teaches that "ordinary people are *not enough*" Robert Johnson writes - and that we should "love people only insofar as they reflect our ideal" - even that "superhuman" or "a dream-woman or dream-man." "As long as people are caught up in this way of thinking," he writes, "they will resist anything but that image, even to the point of "refus[ing] to make a real commitment to a human being, because they will only commit themselves to....the perfect manifestation" of their dream. Subsequently, he continues, "when a flesh-and-blood, mortal human appears in a man's life who offers him love and relatedness, he ends in rejecting her because she can't measure up to that idealized perfection."[18]

As a result, individuals contemplating a long-term commitment can become almost paralyzed: "As long as love is a daydream, they can participate; as soon as it comes down to the reality of the relationship between two real people - they are frozen."[19]

Author Naomi Wolf argues that the basic emotional and physical signals that help us find good partners are "scrambled" by the dominant storyline of attraction: "A woman who is self-conscious can't relax to let her sensuality come into play....If she is 'done up' she will be on the alert for her reflection in his eyes. If she is ashamed of her body, its movement will be stilled." She concludes that if a man's "field of vision has been boxed in" by a narrowed view of 'beauty' - it "prevents men from actually seeing women" - with the possibility that a man may simply "not see her, his real love, standing right before him." [20]

Not seeing

The blindness described here is not simply a metaphorical blindness - but a literal, physical kind, where we *cease to see the actuality of who and what is in front of us*.

Instead of trying to see again, however - we move forward from another break-up to 'put ourselves out there again' and see what kind of other options we can stir up.

If this is 'just how things are,' then we should just keep plugging away. If this is the best we can do, we should just move forward to check out other options...maybe you'll meet someone better next weekend?

But it's not the best we can do. We know it's not. Deep down, our hearts protest! And we know there is another way.

But our minds remain caught up and seduced by the relentless cultural messages around us. Rather than "stimulate and gratify sexual longing" as promised, these can have a "numbing effect" Wolf adds - "reducing all senses but the visual, and impairing even that." [21] As a result, that individual may dwell in a "state of isolation and imprisonment which his lack of love..brought upon him." [22] The tragedy, Johnson writes, is that surrounded with the potential for human warmth and relationship, this person "refuses to enjoy it" instead embracing expectations that cut that person off from "the very love for which he [or she] starves." [23]

That's just what happened to me. The sheer number of crazy ideas about love, attraction, affection - compounded to make it feel virtually impossible to give my heart to someone else.

Of course it wasn't impossible - and of course, there's a better way forward. In the meanwhile, this meandering path can end up hurting pretty bad!

Have you ever walked away from a wonderful match? Have you ever hurt someone deeply...someone who was amazing and beautiful on all levels?

It's usually later that we realize what we've done. "I could have married a girl but chose not to" one man lamented - explaining that he was looking for some other ideal. "Now I look back and think to myself how perfect she is and I realize I blew it."

Most of us don't see this in the moment, however. Instead, we keep our eyes fixed on the task at hand: "Hey, I just haven't met the right person!"

This book raises another strong possibility: What if we *have* met the right person (or lots of right persons), but we haven't been able to see that?

There came a time in my early thirties when I finally confronted myself: Is it true I just hadn't met The Right One - or was something else going on? If I was truly honest with myself, I felt like I had forgotten something important about how to really love.

I knelt down and said one of those rock-bottom prayers made famous by recovering addicts: "I don't know how to do this anymore - but I want to learn how. I really want to change!"

Slowly. Gradually. Convincingly - I saw it. I became it.

In the last half of the book, I'd like to go there.

It's time to de-school ourselves from all the effective training we've received on love and romance. After living in this cultural Petri dish for so long, how about a detox?

I'm no savior - and I'm no guru. I'm just another screw-up, recovering addict - free not from a substance, but from a distracting, delusional story.

And that's the bottom-line for now: Everything troubling we've reviewed so far flows from *one* story, *one* narrative, *one* way of thinking about romance.

Maybe it's time to broaden the conversation. Are you in?

Part Two:

Flirting with a Another Love Story

"Throw away all thoughts of imaginary things."
- Kabir

Chapter 6. Romance Reprised: Another Way

"All the forces in the world are not so powerful as an idea whose time has come." - Victor Hugo

In the first half of the book, we came to a pretty clear-cut conclusion: *something is messing with our love lives.*

I would know - having walked away from a few of the most beautiful individuals in the world.

And I'm not the only one. Thanks to a seductive script and story-line about romance, tens of thousands of wonderful relationship have been hijacked. What starts off as a passionate dream of enduring love turns quickly into a volatile, unsettled, and ultimately evaporating period of occasional affection.

Is this really what we signed up for when we went out seeking the love of our lives? It's hard to imagine anyone choosing this course if they knew what they were getting into.

But they *don't know*, of course. Neither are they aware that they're living out a particular narrative of romance (or that there is any other viable option). You see, when one way of thinking has become dominant, it is *no longer seen as a narrative at all.* Instead, it is Reality - in this case, just The Way Romance Is.

And so all the drama, the heartache, the bruised emotions, the serial break-ups - rather than reflecting suffering that we can learn to avoid - becomes simply The Way Things Are. This turbulence and pain recedes into the background as the inevitable, tragic backdrop on which our ongoing love drama continues to play out. And so it goes: the narrowing of affection, the narrowing of attraction, and the narrowing of beauty all continuing in force - unquestioned and unchecked.

Is this really how it has to be? What if there were a way to reverse some of these heart-breaking relationship patterns so that lasting romance actually stood a chance? Wouldn't that be cool?

Insurrection

'Cool' doesn't even begin to capture it! Imagine couples who are great for each other...*actually staying together*! Imagine the good guys actually liking the good girls (and vice versa).

I call that beautiful. We might even call that a revolution.

Every insurrection begins with a defining event - a galvanizing moment that inspires people to rally. To fight back.

Since the romantic chaos is now happening all around us, there are now hundreds of tragic, galvanizing moments in this revolution - spread out through many of our lives.

Mine came in Manhattan, New York - the beautiful island where I proposed to a truly beautiful woman. Heart, mind, soul - she was as lovely as anyone I've ever met - a being nearly impossible not to love. And we were a fantastic match.

But I just couldn't do it. In the weeks after, I turned away again. Twelve years after devastating my high school sweetheart, I was at it again: Not Feeling It...Not Enough! And therefore, not able - or not willing - to love.

The pain of that moment still tugs at my heart. In the years since, I've witnessed the same kind of blindness repeated all around me in the lives of loved ones and friends, as numerous other relationships are thrown aside.

I will admit, I'm not doing this project as a detached, passive researcher. That's not enough for me. It's revenge I want: revenge against a narrative that brought such despair, such aching heartbreak, and such stunning blindness into my own life - and into the lives of those I've loved (or could have loved).

What's it going to take? I don't know the full answer to that question yet. But I do know the place to start.

Waking up

Rather than incessantly seeking for more, for better, for other options - the place to start this revolution is *wherever you find yourself* - with *whomever you find yourself*.

Immanual Levinas once said, "Truth comes through the face of the other." As we open ourselves to others, we allow their experience, their background, their face - to teach us who they really are.

Even so, we're often "slow to recognize" someone good for us, one author writes, "not because of a shortage of appropriate beings to love - but rather because of the difficulty of attending to them in a manner that enables [us to] recognize them in the first place."

And why is this? For one, the kinds of distractions explored in earlier chapters can effectively prevent us from interacting with someone in a way that allows genuine recognition of who that person really is. This "difficulty of attending," continues this author, may in fact explain "why most of our loves are false starts."[1]

Could improving the quality of our attention towards others, and *seeing* people around us more clearly, make that much of a difference?

You bet. In fact, it might just change everything.

Embracing a human being

What would it mean to lay aside our determined search for a particular face, or form, or feeling, and begin to recognize individuals as they actually are?

Of course, the little details of who someone is are often what trips us up: that mole, that habit, that little glitch...those quinky-dinks that come with our humanity.

But here's the thing: What if we decided that wasn't a problem? What if the other person being a *real human being* didn't have to be a deal-breaker?

For many people, Robert Johnson writes, "It does not occur to them...that a relationship could be made between two ordinary, mortal human beings" who choose to "love each other as imperfect people." Ultimately, he goes on to propose, the "only enduring relationships" happen between couples who embrace this realization. That is "what is required."[2]

What if we we actually allowed people to be human? Rather than trying to become (or find) the most amazingly attractive person, how about just being who we are?

Even one step in that direction - and you know what happens? Just like that - things get simpler. They get easier - and more clear.

Whatever the end of this story, it's beginning place remains reassuringly simple: namely, the face in front of us. "I look around at married [couples] and realize they are not supermodels" one man said with some legitimate surprise: "They are real women and men, he continues - and they are happy!" "Real people, real expectations, and real relationships" - one author emphasized: "Life isn't a well-scripted chick flick," and when we let people "off the hook for not living up to these fictional ideals, we're finally ready for real-life love."[3]

As one author notes "Real love begins only when one person comes to know another for who he or she really is as a human being, and begins to like and care for that human being."[4]

That's not as simple as it sounds in our culture, for sure. Sixty percent of women in one survey said that they wished guys would be more interested in them as a person and less as a sex object.[5] As another writer puts it, "Women wish to be loved not because they are pretty, or good, or well bred, or graceful, or intelligent, but because they are themselves."[6]

Does that really sound so hard?

Diversifying beauty

But of course, it is - it's hard thanks to a surrounding culture that insists we need to be *far more* than we naturally are. So maybe it's time to ask the truly radical question: In a culture that has turned upside down the meaning of love, romance, and beauty, how about turning things right side up? Maybe it's time to start flirting with a different story of romance entirely.

In a recent international study of thousands of women, the overwhelming consensus was expressions of desire "to embrace a conception of beauty that defies the narrow, physically-focused standards set for them by popular culture" - towards a view that is "richer and more complex than the physical ideals that dominate popular culture" and thereby "admits to a far greater and nuanced range of 'the beautiful.'"[7]

In this same survey, for instance, 88% of women strongly agreed that they feel most beautiful when they are happy and fulfilled in their lives. Others mentioned kindness (86%), confidence (83%), dignity (81%), humor (78%) and intelligence (75%) as underlying beauty, with 88% of mentioning a rich spiritual or religious life as expanding their sense of personal beauty.

Being loved (88%) and having a strong intimate relationship or marriage (81%) were other top factors in women feeling beautiful - alongside doing something you love (86%), taking good care of yourself (82%) and having a close circle of friends (70%).[8]

"At the heart of this study is a result which is highly significant," the researchers conclude. That is, "women regard being beautiful as the result of...being loved, being engaged in activities that one wants to do, having a close relationship, being happy, being kind, having confidence, exuding dignity and humor. Women, who are like this, look beautiful. They are beautiful."[9]

When compared with more one-dimensional, prevailing views, this amounts to a radical redefinition of beauty - one centering on more than simply the body. One man spoke of his attraction to his sweetheart shifting from physical qualities to something deeper and broader - a connection expanding to include intellectual and emotional aspects: "attractiveness came to mean all of those things at that point."

One interview participant described observing a woman in the grocery store randomly helping another person in line with a screaming child: "Her whole face lit up as she lifted the child up...you could tell she was happy to be helping. I could see a beauty in her that had nothing to do with what she looked like - a beauty of someone who loves, cares and reaches out to others." One woman writes, "If I were only to seek outward beauty my entire life, I would die incredibly unfulfilled. Beauty is in laughter with friends and family. Beauty comes when we open our hearts to those in need. Beauty is watching the sunrise on your back porch."[10]

From this vantage point, the affection of romance may go deeper than what individuals see alone. "Love is far more than physical attraction" one author writes - "it is deep, inclusive, and comprehensive. Physical attraction is only one of the many elements."[11] Rather than "worry too much about how beautiful or how handsome people are," another writes, "be wise enough to see past that and into the heart and into the spirit of those whom you are dating."[12] A third author notes, "It's never been true, not anywhere at any time, that the value of a soul, of a human spirit, is dependent on a number on a scale....When we start defining ourselves by that which can be measured or weighed, something deep within us rebels."[13]

Instead of de-emphasizing the body, this is about embedding our romantic experiences in a kind of "full spectrum" attraction. Deeper qualities may thus ground love powerfully, with individuals drawn together for reasons far beyond the immediate physical appeal. "Life has taught us that love does not consist in gazing at each other," writes Antoine de Saint-Exupery, "but in looking outward together in the same direction."

It is possible, then, to "think about and experience beauty in complex and dimensionalized ways" concluded the international research team. "To be sure, women want to be physically attractive and they want to be perceived as such." But, they continue, it's also true that "women want to see the idea of beauty expanded."[14]

So what would it mean if we took all of this seriously in our love lives?

A gutsy move

When I realized how narrowly I had typically been approaching people, I decided to try a little experiment myself. Instead of focusing on surface-level attractiveness, I made a conscious choice in social gatherings to focus on what I called for myself, "whole-souled" beauty.

One woman said, "I know many women who are amazing, but because they don't have, say, that perfect figure of what society expects, lots are not given a second chance. They are judged as soon as they are seen. Give someone a chance! There is more to this person - try to find that out!"

As I tried this little experiment, I began to notice things I hadn't before - namely, the people right in front of me. In many individuals I had previously discounted, I began to glimpse richness, intriguing goodness...and yes, stunning beauty. I will never forget the day I noticed several female friends in class ('just friends') - and actually *saw them*...

So how about this as a first invitation - at the next party, gathering, or social event you attend, try this: Rather than moving towards the people you would normally and automatically pursue, stop for a minute and look around at another, deeper level. Who attending the event do you think really has some Full-Spectrum Beauty going on? Whose heart and mind do you find drop-dead amazing? Try starting a conversation with that person. Pay attention to how it goes and what it feels like to be around that person.

I've done this. And with other bachelors I've worked with, I've invited them to try the same.

And you know what happens? Almost immediately, the landscape or 'people-scape' around you can shift.

In my case, I went from being un-interested in going out with anyone in my area to the very next week suddenly noticing *many* people I was interested in getting to know. I can't tell you how shocking this was to me - how unexpected!

Describing her now-husband, one woman said "one of the first times I saw him, he was so skinny and bald that I thought he was dying of cancer." "At that point," she said, "I didn't find him attractive." After spending some time talking with him over several dates, however, things really changed. She explained what happened with her now-husband: "His physical appearance hadn't changed; he was still bald, skinny, white...but his personality, sense of humor and other things started to make him very attractive to me, physically. I started to notice his eyes - his smile started to stand out. To this day, I consider him one of the most attractive men I have met."

That may sound far-fetched...but I dare you: Try it. In your next chance to socialize with people, notice whatever natural inclination you have in approaching people. Then try something different. With Superhero X-ray vision, try looking again at a deeper level: Can you see the whole person - and experiment with an attraction that encompasses everything?

If you're up for this, I'll just warn you: you're moving in the direction of a *much* more profound and lasting romance than if you keep following The Way Things Are Supposed To Be.

Watching for a Good Fit

Rather than going after anyone that stokes passing attraction, our focus now goes to a broader, deeper place - centered around a very different question: *Who out there is a Good Match for me?*

Recent studies have confirmed that love (especially the lasting variety) most often occurs in the presence of fundamental similarities, including common ethnic, social, religious, educational, and economic backgrounds, as well as comparable intelligence, physical appeal, attitudes, expectations, values, interests, and even similar social and communication skills.[15] As one woman wrote of her husband, "We communicate well, we have the same goals, we have the same path, we just fit!"

While there's admittedly a lot of talk these days about compatibility, what does it *really mean* to be well-matched?

In a Biblical language, Adam is recounted as seeking a "help-meet" - defined as someone who is 'meet' (suitable, fitting or appropriate) as a partner. One contemporary philosopher suggests that "love's overriding concern is to find a home for our life and being...to feel at home in the world: to root our life in the here and now; to give our existence solidity and validity; to deepen the sensation of being" and confirm its "roundedness, rootedness" and "at-homeness." The right partner, he continued is someone we experience as "grounding and affirming our own existence."[18]

One woman spoke of "finding a spirit that matches yours." This fit is often a family fit as well. As they say in the Hindu tradition, "Marry someone we can all marry."

Instead of visual-based love at first sight, we're talking here about a love encompassing the whole person - maybe call it 'love at first conversation' (or the 15th conversation?) As Brendan Francis once said, "A man is already halfway in love with any woman who listens to him."

Most people aren't looking for this anymore...at least I wasn't! Instead of a *certain kind of person*, we're often consumed with finding a *certain kind of experience* - e.g., just the right feeling, etc. For this reason, we can end up with surprisingly little notion of what a Good Fit would look like in our own lives.

After seeing how little attention I had invested in finding a Good Match - someone who really "fit" me - I decided to try a another self-experiment. Thinking back through all the people I had met, I wrote out off the top of my head a list of 10 people that I connected especially well with as we spent time together. From that list, I noticed patterns of people who I really jived with.

Try the same thing right now. Thinking over all your past rela-tionship experience, jot down 5 - 10 people with whom you've been able to connect and talk with on a deeper level. Do you see any patterns across these people? Based on this, what would you say a Good Match looks like for you?

When I wrote out my list, one of the first women to come to mind was Monique Moore, a super-fun lunch date from 2 years earlier where we talked about 'everything.' My how-have-you-been e-mail arrived the same day she was moving to back to my city. The rest, as they say, is history.

I'm not making any extravagant promises about your list. But I am saying this: Rather than relying on surface feelings alone, *begin today* to start paying attention to something even more interesting - namely, what does an appropriate match, a Good Fit, look like for you?

If you're anything like me, you haven't really considered this very carefully: What does *your* Good Match think about and care about? What does he or she spend free time doing? How does this person treat other people, including you?

It's time to find someone offering real "grounding" and "at-homeness" in a relationship. You up for this? I'm rooting for you!

Pursuing something *better*

Just for kicks, why don't you try contacting one of those people on your list. It can't hurt...and may actually surprise you!

Do remember, of course, that a Good Match is not the same as a perfect match. This is not about finding some superhuman who meets all core needs at every level.

It's easy enough to then wonder: Does this mean we're settling for something less? Isn't this about giving up something we really want?

The answer to that, of course, depends on *what you really want.* If it's hyper-intense, continually sexually-charged romance you're after - then ignore everything you just read. And just keep doing what everyone in the larger culture says you Should Be doing.

If it's a lasting relationship with enduring, growing romance you want, then yes - it might be time to let go of something. And what is that?

An imaginary ideal. An aspiration that no one actually achieves. A goal that no couple actually reaches.

This is what you're being encouraged to throw overboard.

If that sounds scary, it's okay. Because big changes are sometimes like that.

But don't let that discourage you, because it's all worth it..trust me! As we begin to pursue broad-spectrum attraction, romance and dating becomes a whole new ballgame.

The results may surprise you. One man described many years of looking for someone blond and skinny that fit his ideal, to no avail. Then he met his wife, who was taller, normal-sized and with brown hair. When asked, "Do you realize she is not who you were looking for?" he answered, "It's true...but you know, she is *even more* than I was looking for."

In direct opposition to the narrowing of previous chapters, this is about beginning to pursue *broader* and *deeper* attraction in a partner.

And let's be very clear, this 'other narrative' of love and romance we're talking about is not some attempt to approximate the real deal. This is about *true love* and *genuine, life-lasting romance.*

Rather than accepting something or someone *less*, this counter-insurgent mentality is about embracing something *more* than you imagined - and going gangbusters after a relationship with someone sure to offer genuine comfort and fulfillment.

Good luck. I'm excited for you!

Chapter 7. Broadening: Romance Relieved

"Sometimes it is necessary to re-teach a thing its loveliness,
to put a hand on the brow of the flower and retell it
in words and in touch, it is lovely." - Galway Kinnell

If there is a change needing to happen in our romantic lives, it isn't an aggressive one. No one needs to be 'fixed' from this perspective. Instead, this is about remembering things we used to know - waking up again to something that's already a part of us.

For most of us at younger ages, loving didn't used to be complicated. It wasn't hard. And it didn't hurt.

But sooner or later, that changed for many of us, as we came to feel the heavy touch of a 'love' that was no longer simple. Whether in early chidhood or much later - at some point, love became something else...something complicated, something painful and something we had to fight for and even fear.

Relationships then became hard. And pain in our relationships was something we came to expect. And that's where many of us still find ourselves generally speaking: 'Hey, it sucks - but this is Just The Way Relationships Are.'

This book is interested in what it would take to move decisively towards another place. Is it possible to re-learn again a love that isn't so painful, hurtful or hard?

I believe it is! But it's going to take a different pathway than the one we've been on.

We started down that path in the previous chapter: Full-Spectrum Attraction, diversified beauty, real human beings and a Good Match. As simple as all that may sound, it's so different than what we're Supposed To Be Looking For these days.

What would it mean to take this other story about romance seriously? More than just flirting with the story, what if we started living it out in our actual relationships, moment by moment. What would that look like?

The most immediate and obvious consequence of a new love story is simply this: expectations on relationships aren't so heavy anymore. As couples may loosen their grip on what it's Supposed To Be Like, they allow love, in the words of one author, to "be freed from its long imprisonment by...unreal expectations."[1] For instance, one man said, "When my future wife and I started dating, I didn't feel the same thing about her that I did [in the past] - not the total delirium." Explaining why he continued firm in the relationship, he added, "that's not even sustainable."

So what *is* sustainable? What kind of romantic feeling *can* we count on? After admitting, "I just wasn't feeling 'it' after a recent break-up," one woman said, "I wasn't looking for instant butterflies anymore, but there had to be some 'it' there, right? And if so, how much 'it' was enough?"[2]

Comfortable romance

Reflecting on his decision 40 years ago to marry his wife, one man admitted, "I didn't feel fireworks; I felt completely at ease."

Reflecting on a wonderful relationship she walked away from, one woman said "I just wasn't feeling it - and now I think, what was I *supposed to be* feeling? Because, actually I liked being with him more than any of the guys I felt strong chemistry with before or since."[3]

Is romantic feeling and attraction important? Absolutely. Should it be our all-consuming, overwhelming and defining feature of love? No it should not.

Before all the chick flick aficionados close the book, hear me out! This is no pitch for settling or embracing loveless relation-ships. Instead, we're simply considering here another pathway of progression towards long-term, profound emotional intimacy - one that starts with smaller seeds nourished over time.

Saraceno writes in her historical essay on Italian families about "tranquil affection" as something that used to be widely understood to develop over the course of a long-term relationship.[4] Rather than needing to feel 'everything' right now, a couple may thus look for just enough confirming emotional assurance to begin. Another man who spoke of happily marrying his best friend, said

"Recognize that there's a spark of physical attraction and inter-est...that's all you're going to need. The big stuff comes after years of bonding and working things out."

Does that sound scary to anyone? If feelings are not remarka-bly intense and passionate, why not take that as a sign of mistaken love? And indeed, Johnson writes, "We assume that any other kind of love between couples would be cold and insignificant by comparison."[5]

But is this true? Other cultures offer some additional helpful insights. Couples in eastern societies, one writer notes, tend to "love each other with great warmth, often with a stability and devotion that puts us to shame." But, he notes: "Their love is not 'romantic love' as we know it. They don't impose the same ideals on their relationships, nor do they impose such impossible de-mands and expectations on each other as we do."[6]

This alternative, to be sure, is not something lukewarm like benevolent empathy. Indeed, in life-long companions can be seen a level of love and romance that no movie can duplicate. "You're just comfortable with them," one person said. "Over time, you become comfortable and it doesn't become that giddy as you get inside each others' lives."

In these stories, you can see a deep acceptance of the natural evolution of romance over time: "When two people are first together," one woman writes "their hearts are on fire and their passion is very great. After a while, the fire cools and that's how it stays. They continue to love each other, but it's in a different way - warm and dependable."[7] After describing the "temporary madness" of romance that "erupts like an earthquake and then subsides," another author writes that "love itself is what is left over when being in love has burned away."[8] Compared to the previous or later historical expectations about romance, Coontz notes that during Enlightenment times love was expected to develop "slowly out of admiration, respect, and appreciation of someone's good character."[9]

Rather than needing to be 'madly in love,' 'head over heels,' or find a partner 'the most amazingly attractive person ever,' many couples decide to embrace a romance and love more subtle and potentially more profound. One author writes, "A man reserves his true and deepest love not for [someone] in whose company he finds himself electrified and enkindled, but for that one in whose company he may feel tenderly drowsy."[10]

While being "intimate" is often seen as synonymous with sex, one scientific study identified 5 additional ways of experiencing intimacy and closeness with a partner: Among the various ways to be close and intimate with someone: openness, affection, supportiveness, togetherness, and quiet company.[11]

While there are literally thousands of intense, passionate relationships portrayed around us, there seem to be very few examples of a love that enjoys these others kinds of intimacy. One woman remarked, "Giddiness is discussed a lot...the post-giddiness phase not as much. The expectation gets set from Hollywood, so they think they should always feel that way, but a movie's only an hour and a half - you can only show that [intense] part." However, she continued, "I think that when people get married. they've come to an understanding that they are comfortable and have found a relationship that makes them happy, but they don't portray that [normal comfort] in the media; just the giddy part."

As a result, we come to expect romance as needing to be out of this world. In this chapter, we're saying, "Hey - let's stop doing that!"

While potentially helpful to anyone, this shift in expectations can be especially helpful for those who aren't very emotional or who struggle with relationship connection generally.

Trauma of different kinds in early childhood, for instance, can produce attachment issues that have been shown to predict some aspects of adult romantic relationships.[12] For instance, those with avoidant tendencies are more likely to feel a "generally low level of emotional intensity" in romantic and dating relationships, one study reports.[13] There is also some evidence that our capacity for passion naturally varies as a human population depending on our genetic makeup, with some individuals potentially inheriting the "biological proclivity to fall in love...more intensely than others."[14]

For these people who may feel excluded from the dominant storyline of romance (or beat themselves over the head with others' expectations), this comfortable-romance approach opens another potential pathway to pursue relationships.[15] New expectations thus allow new possibilities and a broader spaciousness within which individuals may explore and love freely - even welcoming the initiation of relationships that would likely otherwise be ignored.

Rather than fulfillment of all-core-needs-at-every-level, this is about finding that meaningful connection or Good Match described earlier. Instead of needing to come to "adore" a particular individual with intense physical/sexual passion - finding nearly everything he or she does amazing and remarkable and stunning and take-my breathe-away all the time - the simple realization here is that *you don't need to be pursuing a demi-god.* Maybe it's time to give yourself permission to relish *another human being.*

Another way of saying this is we don't need to first worship our partner before committing to them.

But hold on: are these expectations really that healthy? If someone is not giddy and 'turned on' most of the time, is that really okay?

This can all start to feel blatantly unromantic - even downright wrong to pursue a relationship in the absence of intense and ongoing amounts of passion.

Rest assured, however - the romance will still be there. "The question" Johnson writes, "is not whether we should praise romantic love or condemn it, keep it or throw it away" - but instead, how to "make a path" of healthy romance and "learn how to honor" the full spectrum of affection.[16]

If this step forward makes things simpler and easier - then why can taking it feel *so dang hard?!*

Physical attraction 2.0

One of the biggest worries (and biggest reliefs) of counter-cultural romance is what it means for the experience of physical attraction itself. As illustrated in an earlier chapter, the criteria for physical attraction have progressively been narrowed to the point of ridiculousness. "The great majority of women" concludes Susie Orbach, researcher at the London School of Economics, find mainstream standards of beauty "too narrow, as inauthentic and as insufficient" - with an aspiration for something much bigger and broader.

As a result, there is a growing movement to "democratize and make accessible to all the idea of beauty" she writes - involving a "redefinition and expansion of the ideals...away from the limiting, narrowed and restricted body shapes and sizes." Orbach concludes, "For the idea of beauty to become truly democratic and inclusive, then beauty itself must be revitalized to reflect women in their beauty *as they really are* rather than as portrayed in the current fictions that dominate our visual culture."[17]

Speaking up "for the beauty of the un-blonde, the un-tall and the un-anorexic," one author writes that "confidence and beauty come in many forms...even the ones our eyes have been trained to forget."[18] "Our results" one research team summarizes, "demonstrate the need to present a wider definition of beauty than is currently available to women. "As we used to know, beauty is so much more," writes lead author Nancy Etcoff from Harvard University:

It is time to "reclaim" beauty...time to lift the quota system on images of beauty. The diversity of human beauty has been strained through a sieve of culture, status, power and money and what has emerged is a narrow sliver of the full panorama of human visual splendor. Ethereal weightlessness and Nordic features are not its only incarnation. Let the discussions and debates begin and let us reclaim and rejoice in authentic, diverse human beauty once again.[19]

While some may be inspired by such words, I have found others taking them to be a threat - reflecting some kind of an assault on physical or sexual attraction itself.

That, of course, is not the case. The issue here is clearly not whether physical attraction is valuable - but *how exactly* to define and approach physical attraction: Shall we embrace a narrow, constricted definition - or one that is broad and diversified?

It's up to you!

Beauty all around

Once beauty, physical attraction and sexual attraction come to be understood in the ways described above, something remarkable happens. Suddenly, beautiful people start showing up all over the place!

In place of a scarcity model that requires mass rejection of most of humanity, this opens up a world of abundant beauty: 'Hey, there are a lot of great people around!' As the large class of 'undesirables' evaporates, the pool of possibilities grows wider and wider. Rather than a select few being given the honor of 'beauty,' this radically "open-access" and democratized approach presents an image of attractiveness wherein *all* can potentially find themselves.

This includes those who don't fit the cultural ideals - for a hundred different reasons: weight, height, symmetry, skin color, age - you name it! Speaking of his elderly wife, one old man related: "I look upon my dear wife, soon to be 92 years of age. I sat at dinner across the table from [her] the other evening. It was fifty-five years ago that we were married...The wondrous aura of young womanhood was upon her. She was beautiful, and I was bewitched." He continued:

> Now, for more than half a century, we have walked together through much of storm as well as sunshine. Today neither of us stands as tall as we once did. Her hair is white; her frame is stooped. As I looked at her across the table, I noted her face and hands. Once [her hands] were so beautiful, the flesh firm and clear. Now [they are] wrinkled and a little bony and not very strong. But are they less beautiful than before? No, in fact, they are more so. Those wrinkles have a beauty of their own, and inherent in their very presence is something that speaks reassuringly of strength and integrity and a love that runs more deeply and quietly than ever before.[20]

Loveliness in its truest sense, then, can grow and expand over time: *getting better*, rather than fading, with age.

In any case, the difference between whether there are "lots of wonderful people" out there or "not many people to date at all," then, may hinge on what exactly we are seeing. Rather than the search for beauty being difficult, the issue becomes: *are we in a place to see it?*

Cultural renegades

Admittedly, within a society preaching the opposite, this view of beauty can be seen with suspicion. One author notes "in a culture where plastic surgery has become nearly as routine as a root canal, the woman who actually likes her body is a rare find. Like an outlaw, she often lives on the fringes of the culture, considered 'odd' because she's not obsessing over her appearance" - instead experimenting with "brave acts of self-acceptance."[21]

Rather than using up the full bandwidth of one's own attention in pleasing others - energy is released to focus elsewhere. "With such fictions removed," one researcher writes, "the many hours of anguish, spent in self criticism, or in the attempt to reshape themselves so that they do in some ways resemble the ideal, have a chance to be freed up and find expression in the many other desires and ambitions that women hold."[22]

Consequently, we may all enjoy life a bit more. "The data," these researchers conclude, "indicate that a deeper, more complex and multi-faceted appreciation of beauty in general may help women feel both more beautiful and happier."[23]

This kind of radical acceptance regarding one's own self, body and experiences can itself contribute to a deepened beauty - as Steve Maraboli stated "There is nothing more rare, nor more beautiful, than a woman being unapologetically herself; comfortable in her perfect imperfection. To me, that is the true essence of beauty."

Broadening expectations

It takes a similar kind of bravery to offer the same radical acceptance to others. One girl spoke of a turning point in finding her life-long love: "I lowered my expectations – not my standards, just my expectations – to a reachable level."

Another person said: "Be willing to step outside of what you think you want. You have this list and it's just not necessary to be happy. Try something new. Light hair, dark hair, who cares? Does he treat you well?...Funny? Smart?...You don't have to have a certain package." One woman said, "There's no way we're perfect in all categories on a checklist, but we might just be perfect for you. Give us a chance."

Women aren't the only ones who need a bigger chance. One man wrote, "a woman broke up with me because she didn't like the clothes I wore - but she's madly in love with a guy who dresses well but doesn't call her." He went on to argue that there were good men out there, but not always recognized as such.[24]

Several of these stories were gathered by Lori Gottlieb, in her fantastic national bestseller, *Marry Him: The Case for Settling for Mr. Good Enough*. Describing her breakup to Lori, another woman said, "He was too predictable." She continued, "Then I started dating guys who always kept me on edge and I never knew what to expect....now I'd give anything for predictable."[25] One author spoke of women she interviewed as "embarrassed by the way they'd dismissed men in the past, evaluating every guy as either too-something or not-something-enough. These guys didn't fit our image of the person we thought we'd end up with, leaving us to end up with nobody."[26]

One woman suggested that people sometimes misunderstand "being realistic as 'settling.'" She continued:

Being open-minded isn't 'settling.' If you really want to get married, then maybe you *should* consider a partner who is less than perfect. For example, a man who makes less money than you, or is a little shorter, or who has been married before, or who is a bit "dorky" isn't the best looking... in other words, all those guys you avoided in your 20s because the dating pool was huge and you could afford to be superficial rather than giving someone a little different a chance.

She continues, "I think that the older you get, the more you have to accept that other people aren't perfect. We get progressively less perfect as life dumps 'experience' (aka, baggage) onto us, so if you're older and still want to get married, I think you've just got to accept that your prospective partner will have as many dings and scratches in their bumper as you do."[27]

Ultimately, overlooking some smaller things on our list can be the difference in whether a relationship ever ends up happening. As David Chambless once said "better to have loved a short man than never to have loved a tall."

Sometimes bigger things may need to be overlooked or forgiven in someone's past. "What's more important," one woman reflected about her partner, "the choice he made 10 years ago or the choices he is making today?'" She continued, "So, I'm not saying settle - not at all" one woman said. "But do a little thinking outside of the box." In the end, one author wrote, discovering someone to "get real with is the true love story."[28]

Stepping in this direction requires detaching from the infinite range of theoretically "better" options that exist. One author said flat out that men and women "have to be *broken* of this 'better one out there' syndrome...*sometime* - e.g., I like you, but I just don't know if it's enough."

The invitation here is to ease up on the expectations we're used to with love and romance - and began to hold them more gently. In the wiggle-room that provides, we can then open ourselves up to real people - in both their strengths and weakness, freckles and birthmarks.

One woman spoke of wanting to shake others and say "the guy who laughs too loud in public may not love the way you chew raw carrots at dinner parties, but it's not a deal breaker for him."[29] Another woman writes, "A good provider may not be a good nurturer. A great thinker may be a sloppy housemate. A caregiver may not be a good wage earner. And a Mr. Fix It may not be your best-looking evening arm piece. Just like you, every man you date is a unique snowflake."[30] Another woman recounted:

When I first started dating David I thought "you are not my type." My type is business man, straight arrow, always done what's right, smart, etc. But when I relaxed and saw who he really was, I realized he was perfectly my type and then all I could think was "how have I not seen how you are exactly my type?" He was perfect for me; it just took a little time for me to see it.

One author writes, "We expect that all our needs will be met and if they don't, something's wrong." She continues, "Nothing's wrong - that's just the nature of two people being in a relationship."[31] One woman advocates looking for "Mr. Good Enough (who exists) instead of Prince Charming (who doesn't)."[32]

As one woman asked, "How long does it make sense to hold out for someone better - whom we may never find, and who may not exist or be available to us even if he did - when we could be happy with the person right in front of us?"[33]

One woman who married one of those "predictable" men said about her relationship: "It is predictable. But it's a lot better than always wondering what was going on with the more exciting guys. That wasn't love. What I have now is love."[34]

Historian Stephanie Coontz suggests that the stability of relationships in previous generations was related to the fact that they were "much more accepting than we are today of a huge gap between rhetoric and reality, expectation and actual experience" in relationships.[35]

Rather than lowering standards, then, we may think of this as an expansion of our acceptance and openness. "I used to chase the girls that all the guys would date - the 12% of girls that are doing 90% of the dating" - one man said. "I have realized over time that no one is going to be a 10 out of 10...but that's ok." He clarified, "I don't think my standards have lowered, but I am more aware of what works for me, and I have actually expanded the types of girls I would date."

More than simply searching for more options, then, this is about revising expectations about those already in front of us: coming to the "right realization" about relationships, rather than just "finally meeting the right girl."

In doing so, we continue to reverse the narrowing process illustrated in earlier chapters - expanding what we mean by beauty so that attraction itself can also broaden. Instead of settling or 'giving up' higher dreams, such a shift can constitute a re-focusing on a radically deeper, diversified beauty as explored above. This, in turn, may cultivate a broadened smorgasbord of options to relish and love.

To be picky or not to be picky: Is that the question?

Comfortable romance, diversified beauty, reachable expectations - are there any lines at all? Are you saying we should let go of our lists - and give everyone a chance?

Not so fast! Having said all this about broadening criteria, it is important to acknowledge there *is* such a thing as settling. Broadening and expanding criteria for relationships, in other words, does not mean abandoning all criteria and standards. One woman said, "I have two younger sisters who settled and I won't do it." Another said, "When it comes to marriage, I'm not going to settle. It's the one area in my life where I'm not going to settle."

This raises a challenging question, namely, what being more realistic actuall *means*: "How much compromise is too much compromise?" one woman asked. And "How do you know if you're being too picky or if you're really not right for each other?"[36]

Rather than simply condemning pickiness, then, the issue becomes *how exactly* individuals ought to be picky (or not) - opening a discussion regarding which expectations are worth retaining and which should be jettisoned.

One woman said, "I've learned...what I don't want and what I'm willing to overlook and not overlook. I've become more aware of what I can overlook. It's okay if his laugh is kind of funny, but it's not okay if he has a porn addiction. that kind of thing." Another woman agreed: "Avoid the big things. If they are addicted to pornography, you should not start that relationship." Another spoke of raising her standards after discovering her boyfriend was doing things behind her back. Another woman said, "The person I end up marrying. how will he treat me in 30 years?"

The point is this: don't forget about the legitimate deal breakers that should still be in place. As one author summarized, "Someone with an addiction, someone who had a bad temper, someone who's unkind, someone who doesn't have a job, someone who's not warm or doesn't have a generous spirit, someone who's inflexible, someone who's irresponsible, someone who's dishonest, someone who wouldn't be a great father [or mother], someone who's old enough to be their own father. The rest...is negotiable."[37]

The confluence of these insights can feel contradictory: 'Be *very* careful who you get involved with romantically' but 'be open and not *too harsh* in your judgments!' Even so, navigating this tension is *possible* - e.g., "to strike a good balance between holding to one's values and things one cherishes the most - not sacrificing those" as one woman articulated, "while at the same time, being flexible and not overly rigid in looking for the perfect person."

At a minimum, this entails holding on to basic expectations for ourselves and those we date.

Beyond 'sup'

"What bothers me," one person wrote, is the "last-minute bailing" and the "lack of forethought...Why should it be acceptable to do everything last-minute?"[38] "Used to be," another researcher noted, "that if women had high expectations and a man wanted her - well, he had to rise to those expectations or move on." Nowadays, by contrast, women "too often respond to a text at 11 p.m. They will put up with the last-minute "'sup?'" calls at 11:30."

Raising even this kind of a simple bar can have an immediate impact. "To hold some power - and advertise yourself to amazing good guys," one author writes, "you need to set the hours when you'll respond to men. The good guys will figure it out and call you." She adds that if he won't call you, he certainly won't make any long-term commitments to you. This becomes, then, a great way to test intentions.[39]

One author writes, "Whenever I meet a woman who holds out to be courted, inevitably she is having better relationships."[40] One woman described expecting a guy who asked for her number to actually call her and arrange a specific activity at a mutually agreed-to time: "Any guy that didn't meet this really, really minimal standard of civility, I just ignored." She continued, "Texting 'wanna hang out?' with no specifics isn't worth replying to. I think it has to do with expectations - if you have them, men will live up to them (and the ones that don't you've screened out)."[41] Another person suggested, "The old dating rituals worked for a reason. Women do want to feel special. It's a wonderful feeling to be pursued and courted by a man." She clarified, "You don't have to go crazy with expensive dinners and red roses...keeping it simple is okay and little gestures do mean a lot." She concluded, "It's not rocket science men - the right woman will reward you for the effort you put into dating. Girls, when a guy is ready and into you - you'll know it. Despite all the bad behavior around us, try not to accept anything less than what you are worth."[42]

Texting or calling is certainly not the biggest issue here. Almost all women interviewed, notes this researcher, "end up 'putting out' early in the relationship (whether they want to or not) and putting up with a certain level of nonsense. All because they think they can't ask for more."[43] For the women who settle, fear of being alone seems to play a strong role, she notes: "I know that fear. I myself had to walk away from more than one relationship before meeting my prince last year. And no, I'm not arguing that doing the right thing will always get you the right relationship you crave. But this much is true: While men are wonderful, we women typically set the standard when it comes to relationships. And...if we set it low, it will inevitably be met."[44] As one woman put it, "Why take a woman out to dinner if she'd just as soon hook up with you and your college buddies at a bar...and is willing to follow you back to your apartment afterward for casual sex?"[45]

From this standpoint, another radical idea emerges.

Drawing a line

You heard me right! Drawing *some kind* of a clear line when it comes to physical, sexual relations can have surprisingly positive consequences. And this isn't coming from a moral or religious basis...just listen to the research. Extensive studies across college campuses by sociologist Mark Regnerus at the University of Texas,

Austin - show that waiting to have sex for the first time increases the chances you'll still be a couple one year later - with 90% of the fast movers broke up before one year.[46] Another researcher at the University of Iowa, Anthony Paik, notes "the longer couples delayed sex, the more exclusive the relationship."[47]

"Taking early sex off the table clears the clouds" writes Wendy Walsh, author of the Love Detox. "It gives you a perspective to make a smart, informed decision." Because your focus isn't the physical, she said, "You two will have time - to talk about your families, your careers, and your life goals."[48] "Early sexual involvement is so overwhelming physiologically and even emotionally that it can cloud the ability to see clearly in these other areas" Dr. Dean Busby notes: "When the onset of a sexual relationship is delayed, it helps couples determine more thoroughly their ability to develop emotional, intellectual, and relational intimacy."[49]

"Having sex early in a relationship - or, worse, before it even starts - is a guaranteed failure," one author writes - "It's just a matter of time. Men won't sacrifice for someone who's easy. They don't work that way." This author goes onto note that "a psychological obstacle makes physical arousal more intense" - citing San Francisco-based psychotherapist Jack Moran, PhD in The Erotic Mind, who explains that partners need "some sort of resistance to heighten arousal and motivate sexual pursuit."[50]

For current or future relationships - give this a try. Go bold. Draw a line - and stick to it. And see what happens.

The pattern is this: waiting in sharing sexual and physically passionate affections prevents a whole lot of heartbreak and increases your chances for a long-term commitment. One self-described playboy said that if women would just hold off in physical intimacies for a time - "they would eliminate 90 percent of the male static in their lives....But women need a wide bandwidth of male attention, so they're too afraid to try it."[51]

These fears are real for both genders - raising the possibility of lost opportunities and even ridicule. Indeed, in this high-supply sexual culture, one author notes, those who "choose to control their output in the marketplace are subtly or overtly pressured to put out." She went on to cite one woman who said: "A guy told me I was frigid. He told me I had a sexual problem because I wouldn't sleep with him." She continued, "He made me feel bad about myself. It was so confusing."[52]

Wendy Walsh challenges people to do a serious "detox" of non-committal relationships, such as "friends with benefits," pursuing in earnest a thorough "love purge."[53] "Women can't control men." Walsh continues, "But women can control themselves long enough to ascertain if a man is a low-risk partner...Give yourself and the men you meet the gift of time. Create some space for him to display his intentions. You owe him that. He's a good guy[...]Giving a man time and space to send you signals about his intentions is a gift to a commitment-oriented guy."[54]

So be strong! This kind of a line and standard, when combined with broadened and gentle expectations overall, can lead to a new and radical possibility for love - a possibility we just happen to be exploring in the very next chapter!

Chapter 8. Fortifying:
Romance Exercised

"The grass is greener where you water it." - Neil Barringham

In some form or another, the same problem has sparked most revolutions throughout history: a lack of freedom.

Of all the consequences of pursuing hyper-intense, continuous passion examined earlier, one of the most troubling is the compulsion and drivenness that can set in with our love lives. If that hyper-intense feeling is there, we're there. Once it leaves, we often leave as well.

This becomes just The Way Romance Is: coming and going quickly, independent of effort, and regardless of choice. And that's just how we explain things as we move forward into relationships (or out of them) independent of effort and conscious choice: "The heart wants what it wants" one person writes. "There's no logic to those things. You meet someone and you fall in love and that's that."

Never mind leading your heart one way or another - just step out of its way! It all sounds so romantic. But is it true?

The choice of love

What if choice does matter to love? What if effort and work in relationships is more than a romance spoiler? What if hearts sometimes do need a bit of leading?

"Love is an activity, not a passive affect," esteemed psychotherapist Eric Fromm writes. "Love and non-love, as good and evil, are objective and not purely subjective phenomena...Love is as love does."[1] He continues, "Even if one is feeling love, if they are not doing anything to help, that person is not loving. If a woman told us that she loved flowers, and we saw that she forgot to water them, we would not believe in her 'love' for flowers. Love is the active concern for the life and growth of that which we love. Where this active concern is lacking, there is no love."[2]

Shakespeare similarly wrote, "They do not love that do not show their love."

Instead of something we primarily feel, love becomes something we do and are. This kind of love is different from a 'feeling of love' - and can be practiced regardless of the level of feeling. The psychologist M. Scott Peck adds, "When love exists it does so.... with or without a loving feeling. It is easier - indeed, it is fun - to love with..the feeling of love. But it is possible to love...without loving feelings, and it is in the fulfillment of this possibility that genuine and transcendent love is distinguished from mere loving of an object."[3]

Instead of simply 'happening' due to spontaneous, hormonal effects, then, love becomes tied to our moment-by-moment decisions and actions. "Instead of following your heart," Stephen Kendrick writes, "you are choosing to lead it." He continues, "The world says to follow your heart, but if you are not leading it, then someone or something else is."[4]

Albert Einstein is quoted as saying, "Gravitation is not responsible for people falling in love." "Love is not an involuntary magnetic attraction or [an] irresistible impulse," Erich Fromm similarly remarked. "To love somebody is not just a strong feeling. True love is an act of will - both an intention and an action...It is a decision, it is a judgment, it is a promise, a commitment and ultimately an art."[5]

The craft of love

Like any kind of craft, then, loving well takes time, patience, and practice. From Plato and Aristotle to Montaigne and Rousseau, sages of history have emphasized that "the key virtues of love need to be learned and trained."[6] Nietzsche himself asserted that love was not a spontaneous emotion that springs ready-formed from us. Instead, all lasting love is ultimately learned: "One must learn to love...we have learned to love all things that we now love...there is no other way. Love, too has to be learned."[7]

And what is it we are learning? To see another human being clearly. In this sense, "The art of love turns out to be very like the practice of Zen or the practice of any Eastern religious art."[8] In this case, rather than practicing feeling, we're talking about a practice in awareness and attention.

How exactly might our awareness need to expand? One author compared a "commitment to passion" with a "commitment to a human being," before suggesting, "in our culture we have these two feelings completely confused."[9] While preserving a wonderful place for passion, something even bigger than passion begins to take its place. At the same time the value of romance is acknowledged, we may come to experience happy, enduring relationships as based on an "anxious concern for the comfort and well-being of one's companion."[10]

To see people as they are: not as an object, but as a human beings with needs as real as our own. How's that for a dare?

Do you sometimes struggle to see the needs of others as real as your own? In the past, have other things like anger, anxiety or other feelings gotten in the way? If you're looking for additional support to move in a better direction, I highly recommend a set of ground-breaking practices developed by the Arbinger Institute - as outlined in Bonds that Make Us Free (the in-depth version) or Leadership and Self-Deception (the quick-read). Check them out! You won't be disappointed.

In comparison to love as a state or condition that happens to you, once again, this underscores love as something we participate in and become. Instead of reflecting underlying feeling alone, "I love you" becomes a verb - an expression of a chosen, ongoing commitment. The phrase "in-love" from this perspective, becomes shorthand for "committed-in-love" or "standing in love."[11]

This radical view features a dramatically strengthened role for basic choice and agency within love. "True love is not a feeling by which we are overwhelmed....Genuine love is volitional rather than emotional," writes best-selling author Scott Peck. "The person who truly loves does so because of a decision to love." He adds, "This person has made a commitment to be loving whether or not the loving feeling is present. If it is, so much the better; but if it isn't, the commitment to love, the will to love, still stands and is still exercised."[12]

Ultimately, this highlights a redefinition of love itself. Scott Peck writes: "Love is not a feeling. Many, many people possessing a feeling of love and even acting in response to that feeling act in all manner of unloving and destructive ways."[13]

Finessing the feeling?

So how is this any different than saying we need to just 'try harder to feel loving' and exercise more will-power: 'Hey, what's your problem? Why don't you just choose to love that person?'

Is that what this is about? It's easy to jump to scary conclusions about the role of effort in love: "I've lost the ability to BS myself" one person told me "to cheat myself into feeling I'm in love with someone."

Me too! I don't know anyone who has mastered that strange skill: 'Hey, let's work on this together until we feel enough!'

Of course that doesn't work! As Catharine Sedgwick wrote in 1819 to explain why she broke off an engagement, "It is impossible for me to create a sentiment of tenderness by any process of reasoning, or any effort of gratitude."[14]

"Working harder at love" is not what we're talking about here - nor am I suggesting you try and 'make yourself feel' something you don't feel right now.

Instead of choosing to feel something, the invitation here is about choosing to *practice something*.

Practicing love

There are lots of valuable things that don't come easy or quickly or automatically - think swimming or baseball or piano or singing or public speaking or meditation.

In each case, we use the word "practice" to describe what we do to increase our ability: focused, dedicated, mindful attention towards a growing capacity in these areas.

But does that really apply to love and romance? Most of us certainly don't think so. As described earlier, the experience of love is assumed to come readily, easily and even automatically. Barbara Lee Fredrickson writes about how she used to see love as this "constant, steady force" that defined her relationships. "While that constant, steady force still exists," she continued, she now sees her relationship bonds "as a product of the many micro-moments of positivity resonance that my husband and I have shared over the years."

She went on to describe a study her own research team at the University of North Carolina conducted to put this kind of "love practice" to the test. One group of people randomly assigned to practice creating more "micro-moments of love in daily life" showed enduring improvement in the function of the vagus nerve which connects the brain and heart. Other studies have documented an impact of this same kind of loving practice on healthier immune cells: "Your immune cells reflect your past experiences of love"[15] she writes.

These kinds of "small emotional moments" Fredrickson concluded, "can have disproportionately large biological effects" - especially over time. There's a feedback loop at play, she points out: "Your micro-moments of love not only make you healthier, but being healthier builds your capacity for love. Little by little, love begets love by improving your health. And health begets health by improving your capacity for love."[16]

If you're looking for a simple, and effective guide to increase 'micro-moments' of love in a particular relationship, there are a number of helpful, hands-on guides available. The one I'm most familiar with is <u>The Love Dare</u> *series by Kendrick and Kendrick. This book lays out 40 days of mini-exercises one partner tries each day (without the other person knowing). For instance, "contact your partner sometime during the business of the day. Have no agenda other than asking how he or she is doing and if there is anything you could do for them."[17] If you're aware of other similar guides, I would love to share them with other readers - so please send them my way!*

Once again, this is not about 'working' our way to love. Instead, we're talking about making sure we position ourselves to receive the love already available to us. If love is a gift, are you ready for it?

No matter the details of our effort, the point is this: feelings of love (which we cannot simply choose) may develop over time as we begin practicing some of these fundamentals of love. Moment by micro-moment, we can move slowly, but surely, in a direction that can increase our own feelings of love for someone over time.

What if we approached our love and romance like this: as a practice - like meditation - that we may not be good at initially, a practice that we never perfect, but we keep practicing anyway?

Dad gets married

I was lucky to grow up in a home where Mom and Dad loved each other. Like most couples, they had some real differences in personality and interests, and passed through their own challenging times. Through it all, they kept at it - 'practicing' love throughout the years of their marriage.

I didn't fully grasp how significant this was until after Mom was gone - passing away in 2012 to cancer at a relatively young age. Dad's mourning was profound - a visceral gut-check that brought him to tears almost daily. Mom had encouraged him to find another partner after she died, so after a period of time he began dating.

By that point, I had witnessed hundreds of dates from friends, classmates and bachelor roommates. The majority of first dates, of course, ended with one or both people reaching a resounding 'meh.' And when couples actually started dating, the hot-and-cold uncertainty, drama and heartbreak were so ubiquitous that it was easy to believe this was Just How Dating Was - at least until you have found the Right One.

But then I watched my father. As he went out on one date, then another, Dad came home dumbfounded by the different women he was meeting: 'She's remarkable!...Wow, she's so lovely...I can't believe she hasn't been snatched up.' While not every date worked out, *every woman* had a beauty that Dad could see.

The contrast with my bachelor friends couldn't have been more profound. What my father saw everywhere seemed to be almost invisible to some of my guy friends. I started joking that Dad should start giving seminars on dating to older bachelors (I wasn't really joking).

After a number of dates with several women, Dad eventually sought to date one of them on an exclusive basis. He courted Ann for a couple of months, then moved forward and proposed marriage.

And boom! Then they got married. Just like that.

Does that really sound so hard? As I reflected one day on what made Dad's experience so much smoother than the norm, it hit me: "You shouldn't be surprised that your dad knows what true love is. He's been practicing it for 38 years!"

Deeper than feeling

So what does that look like? As you've already heard by now, throughout most of my experience, I pursued and sought relationships based primarily on what I felt like. For years, I sought the kind of feeling that compelled and drove me together with someone. Far from being reckless, this seemed the most obvious and sensible way to proceed in choosing someone to date.

But something began to change - especially after witnessing the death of some truly beautiful relationships. I couldn't keep doing the same thing I was doing. I started to seek what I wasn't grasping.

My first major realization was this: We are more than what we're feeling, moment by moment. We are also what we're thinking...what we're aware of...what we value and believe and relish.

Once I realized this, I began to look to something deeper than feeling alone to guide my relationship decisions. Instead of being driven by immediate, overwhelming physical attraction, something broader and deeper began to fuel my love life. This may mean the difference in the survival of a relationship at certain critical times.

One woman who struggled with bipolar depression underscored this point: "I cannot have 'love as a feeling' as my answer, since I can't trust them [my feelings]. They change all the time. I can't base my relationship on a feeling!"

In a way, this is no different than what someone facing serious depression or anxiety must do - namely, discover that there is something *deeper* than feeling and thought: something to which they can anchor themselves, no matter what the feelings and thoughts may be like.

My neighbor got engaged to a girl several years ago - the kind of couple that *everyone* knew was an incredible match. But he started having lots of anxious thoughts hitting him rapid-fire. He decided he would start doing all these things - memorizing positive thoughts, reading books, to make the anxiety *go away.*

I told him "Please stop! All those frenetic efforts to *make yourself feel the right way*...this could be making things worse." From that point, he started to explore a more mindful path to relate to these crazy thoughts differently, and he found himself able to move forward.

The point is this: We do not have to be tyrannized by our feelings - whether depressed feelings, anxious feelings, not-sure-if-I-like-her-enough feelings, or self-absorbed feelings.

We can watch them. We can note and study them. Then we can decide what direction we want to go - at our core - whether this means yielding to those feelings or letting them pass.

But this takes practice...and some guts! In the case of my work with people facing depression/anxiety, some excellent exercises exist that can help us learn to approach crazy thoughts and feelings from a deeper place [see *The Mindful Way Through Depression* (2007) by Williams et al. to learn more - or check out an online class, "Mindweather 101," that my colleagues and I have put together to help people learn this same approach - available at www.alloflife.org]. Those same exercises can definitely also help with relationships - alongside other kinds of practices cited elsewhere (e.g., *Bonds that Make Us Free, The Love Dare,* etc).

What we really want

As a result of the foregoing, we begin to live out of a much deeper place. Instead of *The Feeling* driving our relationship decisions day to day, we may be led by commitments that are also more stable and profound - judging relationships in light of what we believe, what we most deeply want and what we fundamentally know.

I was also surprised to discover that what I *most deeply wanted* didn't always align with my current feelings. The *feeling of what we want* can vacillate and change, moment by moment, depending on fluctuations in our body and circumstances. Depending on whether partners are angry or calm, their immediate feeling of what they want in a relationship may change. The same is true for passing moments of sadness, anxiety or lust. As long as one's decisions hinge or center on these feelings, life (and relationships, especially) will be quite a ride (and not the fun kind).

But when love decisions center on something more than the *feeling of what we want*, things can stabilize considerably. If, instead, we base choices on what we *really want*, we can chart a calm and constant course - and this, in whatever direction we truly and most deeply desire. When feelings of anger or sadness or anxiety or lust arise, that course will not suddenly change. And when those same feelings pass (as they always do), we will still be on the same course we really wanted - rather than taken off on some tangent that felt exciting at the time.

That's definitely not how I was approaching romance. In good relationships that I abandoned, I did so out of a desperate commitment to possessing intense romantic feeling. That was my litmus test.

I found out the hard way that by positioning hyper-intense romantic feeling as the all-powerful deal-breaker, beautiful possibilities are killed. By contrast, if the feeling-du-jour is not necessarily Reality, but instead simply, the *feeling of the day* - then a bit of space opens up. They cease to tyrannize us. We cease to cower in submission.

As conflicted feelings are approached more skillfully, we may notice space to work with even finer distinctions in emotions. One man spoke of breaking up three times due to the "bubbling feeling...fading" - with a girl he eventually married. He writes, "On the fourth try I realized that it was fear and worry that I was feeling, not the absence of love."

All of this becomes a whole lot easier when we get clear about the connection between feelings and identity itself. If feelings are taken to be an unerring reflection of self, identity or Reality, it makes sense that resisting them would be at best, uncomfortable and at worst, pathological. If, however, feelings are understood to come and go, sometimes reflecting Reality or self, other times not - then approaching them thoughtfully and critically would make good sense.

Even so, the thought of disobeying one's feeling in any degree, can be scary - after all, 'This is how you feel: are you going to be stupid enough to *deny* that?' Aren't we supposed to be true to what we're feeling? Aren't we crazy to move forward if we don't feel intensely about someone?

Following the peace

All these questions, of course, are enough to send any one of us scurrying away from relationships - if there is nothing else to anchor us.

But there is. In relationships between two well-matched individuals, there is not always delirium, continuous exhilaration or mind-numbing pleasure. Good relationships, like good airplane flights, may still have to face real turbulence before reaching their destination.

But beneath all the feelings and fear is another level entirely - a deeper place from which we can observe everything else happening. On that level, there lies something else beyond the rhetoric and propaganda about what romance Should Be - our own felt sense of comfort and peace (or not).

In the relationships I abandoned, for instance, it was not for a lack of peace. Even with the fears of not-feeling-enough that arose, there was often still a peace in these relationships at the beautiful possibilities between us.

This peace later became the crucial variable, the 'dealbreaker' for whether a relationship should continue. Rather than making decisions based on presence or lack of romantic thrill alone - I focused more on this deeper sense of peace and attunement as to whether to move forward (or not).

Whatever decision is made, we're no longer just letting our feelings drive us anymore. Rather than giddiness, excitement or other emotions alone, an assurance in deeper realities takes over. It is peace we're looking for.

Of course, peace (or lack of peace) can lead you away from someone - just as much as it can lead you towards them. But when the feelings change and romance settles a bit, rather than automatically jumping ship, a decision can emerge grounded in individual choice, judgment, peace...and romance.

In its betrayal of the dominant storyline, a romance along these lines can take some guts. One woman recollected one older friend telling her that "she and her husband weren't 'in love' when they got married, they just knew it was right." She continued:

As an overly romanticized teenager I couldn't even believe such a thing could happen, much less be shared with other people. The whole thing sounded awful. But now I look back and remember that couple as one of the most loving couples I have ever met. They said they always felt peace from the beginning, just not the roller coaster ride giddiness so often portrayed in the movies. However, as they allowed the relationship to progress over time, the love did too.

As reflected here, no one's asking you to walk away from the possibility of romantic love. Instead, this is about considering another way of pursuing and embracing romance in its fullest scope. As illustrated in the account above, feelings of attraction can still play a meaningful role without dominating or driving individuals. Romance is also still there - intermittently at the right times - and alongside other factors playing an even more powerful role.

Progressing in relationships, in this sense, requires a kind of confidence and faith in the person you are with - and in your potential together. Fromm writes, "Love is an act of faith, and whoever is of little faith is also of little love."[18] Beginning and carrying on a healthy relationship take plenty of trust, one man said: "at its beginning and along the way every relationship takes leaps of faith."

Beyond poor matches

One of the biggest leaps of all is walking away from someone that's not good for you: "All I could think about was her...I would wake up with physical pain, literally, in my stomach...I had a really hard time getting over her... it was so painful to realize that we couldn't be together." He continued, "I received a very strong answer and spiritual impression which solidified things...that things wouldn't work out."

The good news is that as we pursue an individual that satisfies deeper feelings and broader criteria, the wrong matches stand out. This does not mean, of course, that it is necessarily easier to walk away. As many of you well know, this may at times wrench your very heart-strings - especially when you're walking away from someone amazing. I once met a remarkable woman, and fell head over heels in love - Hollywood passion all over the place. Very soon, however, I began to have terrible feelings that it was wrong. For whatever reason, I couldn't feel peace...not even on a run, not even meditating. The tension between the romantic passion and the internal dissonance was excruciating.

So with all the strength I could muster, we told each other that if we really loved each other, we wanted the person right for us. We kissed and said goodbye. This was the absolute hardest moment in my life - nothing before or since has hurt half as bad. But having the courage to do this was crucial to be led towards the right (and better) relationships for each of us.

All right - I've got to say it. If you currently find yourself in a relationship in which you can't find peace, reach deep inside of yourself and love that person enough to let them go.

One man said, "Too often, I would stay because I didn't want to break her heart. it took years to realize the need to get out of a relationship as something far more constructive than staying to avoid the heart-break. Get out of a relationship if it's not the right one - don't stay in a relationship for charitable purposes or selfish purposes. If you feel you should get out, get out."

Embracing great matches

Okay, so enough about avoiding poor matches. What about the good ones?

The same broadening that helps us better recognize poor matches can also open our eyes to the subtle signs of an excellent fit. One woman said, "I always knew when I heard 'this relationship is different,' that there was a good chance it was heading toward marriage. They described the difference as peace, not exhilaration; comfort not infatuation. I watched these relationships grow into solid, loving relationships that lasted and they are still some of the happiest friends I know."

On another occasion, I felt lots of peace with an amazing girl, but not all the intensity I thought I was Supposed To Feel. And yet the deepest part of me gently, quietly drew me on: 'Move forward - things will be great.'

What we decide in that moment makes all the difference. *What will you do?*

Chapter 9. Enduring: Romance Undeterred

"It is hard for us to imagine that there could be any love, at least any worthwhile love, still alive for a couple after romance departs." - Robert Johnson

There are many choice-points in any developing relationship - key moments that determine what trajectory the relationship follows.

Of all the potential moments a couple faces, there is arguably none more crucial or impactful than the one at the heart of this book: the great settling-of-the-feeling!

For any who have experienced it, the experience of falling in love is one of the most thrilling experiences of life. As feelings of intimacy and closeness emerge, it becomes easy to imagine one's own needs "entirely met in another person in a 'fantastic unity' where 'the future will all be light.'" [1]

But no matter the relationship, no matter the excitement, no matter the passion, inevitably comes the moment when the "spell is broken." Sooner than later for all couples, "inexorably, reality intrudes" as the "problems of normal living arise." [2] More often than not, as the two individuals become better acquainted, "their intimacy loses more and more of its miraculous character." [3]

This shift is often discussed and even expected in marriage. There is much less conversation, however, about what it means when it happens in dating relationships. Whatever the circumstances, this shift in feeling can "pull most of the artificial intensity out of relationships" and "things will seem quieter and less exciting" as "the dance quietly fades." This change can feel excruciating, shocking and damning - all at the same time. [4] What then?

The easiest route, of course, is just to go where most people go: *"Red flag, bad sign - I'm not getting what I deserve...If The Feeling isn't as intense anymore, something must be wrong!"*

Maybe? Maybe not. It's definitely possible, for instance, that more time leads you to see some fairly serious concerns that you didn't notice before - things you should *not* overlook. Maybe the person doesn't actually treat you very well - getting angry pressuring you, demeaning you. Maybe the person shows some signs of an addiction to alcohol, drugs or sex. These should be non-negotiable issues.[5]

But you already know that - and couples breaking up because of these issues is not really my interest here.The thing that launched my own searching was not legitimate break-ups - it was *all the other couples* - the ones that everyone else can see "would be great together"..."I hope it really works out"..."She's an amazing girl"..."He's just incredible"...but alas!

To any who may be wondering about this kind of relationship now - or any who have walked away from someone in the past who was a great match - please hear me out. Because the _very moment_ when a relationship is being hit the hardest by similar fears could turn out to be a great opportunity - maybe even, your "finest hour."[6]

The war begins

The fateful moment begins as soon as the romantic feelings start to settle. In this moment, we begin to hear a "whispering that 'true love' is somewhere else, that it can't be found within the ordinariness" of this relationship. This voice tells us that "life will only have meaning if [we] go after" that romantic intensity again - "Nothing less will do, for [you deserve] passion, and passion is all." "You must seek this passion" - no matter the cost. We have a "'right' to fall 'in love'....that is what life is all about!" It is our "affirmative 'duty'...to get all the excitement and intensity that we can."[7]

We begin to wonder if their relationship was right in the first place - or begin to focus on small negatives as points of resentment. Mannerisms or facial features that used to be irrelevant become new evidence that 'I'm not getting the experience I deserve.' Those who hang on can see themselves as martyrs - with continuing in the relationship seen as sacrificing one's happiness and losing one's chances for true love. At this point, Johnson writes "it is hard for us to imagine that there could be any love, at least any worthwhile love, still alive for a couple after romance departs."[8]

Indeed, in this mindset , it's hard not to desperately miss the ecstasy and rush. It's hard not to feel as if we are "cheating" ourselves if we continue on in the relationship - "giving up" on something we really wanted - and "something that excited and thrilled" us.[9]

In light of these pulls and tensions, Johnson writes "suddenly our human loyalties...are going in different directions ..in a terrible conflict of values." And then: "one day he meets a woman who catches [his eye]..."He knows nothing of her...he only knows that this 'other woman' seems like the essence of perfection; a golden light seems to envelop her, and his life feels exciting and meaningful when he is with her."

"On that day," he continues, "two opposing armies in the Western psyche take up their swords and go to war" inside us.[10] On one hand is everything good experienced and felt in a relationship - including commitments, memories, peace and whatever potential you've glimpsed - each of which calls for more hope and patience. On the other hand, a voice continues "insisting fervently that it is a wonderful thing to search" more for something better - ..."rather than settle for the flesh-and-blood [individual] that real life has put into [our] arms."[11]

"Unfortunately," Johnson continues, "it is exactly at this point in our evolution, where our possibilities are richest, that most people miss their opportunity...and jump to the wrong conclusions." One or both partners begin talking about breaking up "in order to 'find themselves.'" At this point, we decide that "it is clear that a dreadful mistake was made, we misread the stars, we did not hook up with our one and only perfect match, what we thought was love was not real or 'true' love, and nothing can be done about the situation except to live unhappily ever after [or separate]."[12]

For a man in this situation, the focus is on what his partner lacks: "She is not making him happy; she is not good enough; she does not fulfill his dreams....He always assumes that somewhere, in some woman or in some adventure, he is going to find" what he is looking for - and "be able to...find there his meaning and fulfillment."[13] "In order to be true to the inner ideal" Johnson writes, individuals may feel compelled to walk away: being "faithful" to their ideal - by betraying their current partner.[14]

Embracing evolution

Rather than fearing this change in romantic feelings and emotions - what if we did something else instead? What if we watched these emotions, this shift - as mentioned earlier. What if we watched them long enough to understand and accept that *it is in the nature of feelings to change* - to ebb and flow and evolve over time.

Contemplative writers sometimes talk of "mindweather" - reflecting the way thoughts or feelings can change, moment-by-moment, like weather patterns or clouds passing in the sky. Some days, our mind-weather is sunny - everything is easy and unusually calm. Other days, the storm hits, for no apparent reason. The nature of our emotional experience, for most people and most days, can fluctuate for many varied reasons.

The point is this: Whether ebbing or flowing, emotional change can be expected. Feelings change - they all do. And they do it all the time. Rather than it being a bad sign or indicator that love was "not meant to be," this emotional fluctuation may simply reflect that "feelings...are shallow, fickle and unreliable" and "can fluctuate depending upon circumstances."[15]

If this is true for emotional experience generally, it's certainly not what we expect for romance. As indicated above, there is instead a sense of "Oh, too bad...it's unfortunate the intensity has passed," like it's an announcement of sad news.

What if romantic feeling doesn't follow a set of special rules? What if it actually works a lot like all the rest of our emotional experience?

The type of love experienced in "sudden intimacy," Erich Fromm writes, is "by its very nature not lasting" and "short-lived."[16] Scott Peck states:

> The experience of falling in love is invariably temporary. No matter whom we fall in love with, we sooner or later fall out of love if the relationship continues long enough. This is not

to say that we invariably cease loving the person with whom we fell in love. But it is to say that *the feeling* of ecstatic lovingness that characterizes the experience of falling in love *always passes.*[17]

For any couple, one journalist writes, The Feeling of intense romance, "does not last very long and cannot if lovers are ever to get anything done[...]The passion ignited by a new love inevitably cools and must mature into the caring, compassion and companionship that can sustain a long-lasting relationship" - reflected in "deep affection, connection and liking."[18] Dr. Lyubomirsky, researcher at the University of California, Riverside, likens the decline of this passion to growing up or growing old - in other words, simply part of being human.[19]

The natural changes in romantic emotion over time have been confirmed over the years by many research studies that have documented processes like, "saturation, reduction of uncertainty, tolerance, the law of changing emotions," and "hedonic adaptation."[20] These well-known physiological, psychological, and interpersonal processes capture the normal way that intense states of early love slowly change and turn into something different as the relationship develops.

If both members of a couple can accept these changes as something natural, rather than traumatic, of course, it can mean the difference between relationship life or death.[21]

If love were just a feeling which comes and goes, this would naturally disallow any sort of permanent commitment over one's life: "If love were only a feeling, there would be no basis for the promise to love each other forever."[22]

But what if feelings are *supposed* to evolve - not as a problem, but as a healthy part of relationship development? From this vantage point, when the intensity subsides, "you have to make a decision" one author writes. At that point, you have to "work out" whether individual roots have become "entwined together" enough to continue: "Because this is what love is. Love is not breathlessness, it is not excitement, it is not the promulgation of promises of eternal passion....Love itself is what is left over when being in love has burned away."[23]

If feelings subside, individuals may not, therefore, necessarily distance from each other automatically. Instead, it launches another phase of a relationship where a couple learns how much love they are willing to give.

No matter the decision, we move forward understanding that love is more than a feeling. And so rather than watching breathlessly whether feeling is 'there' or 'not' and getting upset when a shift happens, we can stand comfortably on more settled ground. From this place, we may appreciate the rich spectrum of evolving emotions over time, noticing how romantic feelings evolve over different seasons and for different reasons. The newness of an early relationships, of course, can stimulate romantic feelings simply because novelty raises dopamine activity[24] - what Scott Peck calls a trick Mother Nature plays on us to get us together.[25] More broadly, any period where overall closeness and intimacy is changing has also been shown to stimulate greater passion.[26]

Lifestyle habits can also play a role - with drug use potentially altering the structure and function of the brain's reward system for weeks, months, or years.[27] One research team suggests that "antidepressants can jeopardize one's ability to feel romantic passion for a new partner or a deep attachment for a long-term mate" - specifically, by suppressing dopaminergic pathways, dulling emotions and reducing sexual desire. They relate the account of a man, who said: "After two bouts of depression...my therapist recommended I stay on antidepressants indefinitely. As appreciative as I was to have regained my health, I found that my usual enthusiasm for life was replaced with blandness. My romantic feelings for my wife declined drastically." With the support of his therapist, he continued, "I gradually discontinued my medication. My enthusiasm returned and our romance is now as strong as ever."[28]

Overall, this view acknowledges there are times when we feel little affection or love - even for someone truly precious to us. Sooner or later, we all learn to navigate the calming and settling of feelings - at least if we want any kind of enduring, rich, relationship. Rather than a threat, this can be embraced as a natural evolution of any lasting relationship: "We are not the same persons this year as last; nor are those we love" W. Somerset Maugham writes, adding that happiness comes "if we, changing, continue to love a changed person."

Loving more

So what exactly does this all mean for the problem of fading passion?

Emotions change naturally - including romantic ones. We get that. That doesn't mean we have to *like it* though, right? I mean - isn't it still kind of a problem when the romance settles?

That's precisely what we usually think. When the sweet excitement of early intensity fades, one author writes, that is often "the moment of disillusionment. You think love is gone...This is the time that most people go back and look for someone else to provide this feeling of euphoria."[29] Another author notes, most "react to this stage of romantic love - this breaking of the spell - as though it were a great misfortune!" - even a "disaster": When a man's intense feelings for a woman "unexpectedly evaporate," this author continues, "he will often announce that he is 'disenchanted' with her; he is disappointed...[and] acts as though she had done something wrong."[30]

By contrast, Johnson continues, this moment may be seen as "the crucial point in an evolution," the opening of an "awesome possibility." Up to that moment, we've been approaching this person because we're getting a lot out of the relationship. Our giving to that person can be motivated, in large part, by the passion, intensity, and excitement coming back to us. In that sense, our 'love' during that time can be fairly self-centered.

Then the bottom appears to fall out: less excitement, less passion, less intensity. How could that not be a tragedy?

Here's how. You're now ready (hopefully) for love's greatest test. You are now being asked to love this person not primarily for what you're getting out of it - but for that person alone. Scott Peck proposes "real love often occurs in a context in which *the feeling* of love is lacking, when we act lovingly despite the fact that we don't feel loving. It is when a couple falls out of love [that] they may begin to really love." He later adds, "True love happens *after* the love starts to fade."[31]

Did you catch that? This very moment in which you see this imperfect human being by your side, in which maybe you are *not* getting *everything* you want from a relationship - this very moment, rather than a crisis or a tragedy, could actually be the moment you get to start loving them for real - not because you're driven to, but because you choose to be there. Rather than a crisis, this is an *opportunity* to begin *practicing real love.*

Seeing truthfully

Pretty cool stuff! When feelings settle, then, rather than taking that as a sign of 'not loving you anymore' - or 'not being right for each other' - exciting new possibilities arise. Beyond the natural illusions of early love, an individual now "has the chance to see the woman he loves.. as she is, to relate to her and value her as a person."[32]

Researchers at UCLA and the University of Texas, Austin have found that whereas all new couples have a general, global appreciation of each other - only some couples are able to affirm each other on the level of detail. Those partners who are able to extend love while still recognizing both positive and negative qualities, practice a form of "compassionate love" that has a much higher chance of long-term relationship satisfaction: "the compassionate lover does not gloss over the partner's specific negative qualities, but rather holds the partner in high esteem while at the same time acknowledging specific faults and weaknesses."

By contrast, "consider that if individuals truly believed that every specific aspect of their partners was fabulous, then loving them would not be very difficult" they continue. And admittedly, "some spouses may not be able to love their partners unless they view each of their partners' specific traits very positively." In this case, they write, "once the partner's less-than perfect traits come into awareness, the spouse's love for the partner may dissipate."

These researchers conclude, "understanding and accepting a partner's specific strengths and weaknesses may represent a selfless act, in that spouses endure the costs of their partner's faults, weaknesses, and limitations but love them anyway. In other words...these spouses are unconditionally valuing their partner at a fundamental level."[33]

Rather than being driven to and fro by a feeling, then, this kind of love is grounded in many deeper realities - including the person in front of us! As one author notes beautifully, "Love is a presence."[34] More specifically, this takes love beyond simply a warm feeling for one's partner (which is nice when it happens) - towards a "love founded on an accurate understanding of the partner."[35] This kind of love that sees the other person clearly, fully and acurately - including in the details - proves itself much stronger over the long-term.[36]

To review, then, the "breaking of the spell" mentioned earlier, "opens a golden opportunity to discover the real person who is there...opening the possibility of relating to a woman as an individual, as an equal, as a being in her own right. It enables him to begin to know her as she is, in all her complexity, in all her strengths and gifts - so different from his own."[37]

That can be a very scary moment - no joke...when peace *defies* what the world around is telling you you're Supposed To Want...What will you do when that happens?

Hopefully we can accept another person as "a human being rather than the embodiment of [our] fantasy." This might allow us to "graduate" from reliance on grandiose images of each other into a mature, authentic relationship. Once again, relationships in other cultures provide an example. Johnson elaborates:

In the traditional Hindu marriage, a man's commitment to his wife does not depend on his staying 'in love' with her....His relationship to his wife is based on loving her, not on being 'in love' with an ideal...His relationship is not going to collapse because one day he falls 'out of love,' or because he meets another woman who catches his [interest]. He is committed to a woman and a family, not to a projection.[38]

"We think of ourselves as more sophisticated than the 'simple' Hindus" Johnson notes. But by comparison, the average Western individual is like "an ox with a ring in his nose" - following idealized images around from one person to another and "making no true relationship or commitment to any."[39]

All this can change, however, when we walk away from the ox-nose-ring story of romance. When this happens, these moments of settling and fading can lead to a very different outcome.

Still right here

I grew up watching a mother and father dance to Karen Carpenter in the kitchen and loving each other in a hundred different ways. Then at age 40, Mom was diagnosed with cancer. Over fifteen years of treatment, her body became frail - more like an older woman. Periods of depression and anger swept over her as well.

How did my father respond to this all? He loved her *more* - and made sure she felt cared for her *even more*.

A lesser man would have walked away...but Dad stood up.

Is this just an unusual, rare example? Or could the rest of us have this in us as well? Why not find out?

We certainly don't have to wait for years of marriage to show this kind of love. There are times in *every* relationship, when we feel little affection or love - even for someone truly precious to us. But the true marker of true love is this: the turbulence *doesn't change things.*

In the thousands of years love has been discussed, one of its most widely-known definitions is the Apostle Paul's in the book of Corinthians. No matter how someone feels about the Bible, it's interesting to note the pattern in his language describing love. According to Paul, love "beareth all things, believeth all things, hopeth all things, endureth all things," is "not easily provoked" and "never faileth."

One test, perhaps *the* test of whether you love someone, is what do you do when challenges start to come and The Feeling starts to settle. Do you bolt? Do you leave them high and dry when feelings change?

Or are you unmoved? Are you there for them - still seeing the person, the future together, the beautiful possibilities?

One marker of true love, from this vantage point, *is that it lasts. It doesn't go away...it doesn't fade. It doesn't stop calling. It doesn't stop. It fails not.*

In graduate school, I met one woman who had been married to a man I knew. He contracted a serious degenenerative disease and it was too much - she walked away. I loved this friend - and not knowing all the circumstances, withheld judgment. But as this man devolved in health - every time I saw his ex-wife, I couldn't help feeling a pang of sorrow - at what she had missed out on. The opportunity she had missed to love truly.

Therapist Stanton Peel proposes that the "responsibility for selecting and nurturing a love relationship" is what "actually defines our humanity."[40]

And yet in the world in which we live, this kind of love has increasingly become a rare and singular art. As Erich Fromm wrote decades ago, "the attainment of the capacity to love...remain(s) a rare achievement."[41]

What if we bucked this trend - and added ourselves personally to the 'endangered species' list called lasting commitments? Make it your own little experiment. If you're experiencing relationship difficulties (especially the Not Feeling Enough kind) - allow yourself to stick with that person for a longer period time than you normally would, courageously pursuing some things to make the relationship better. Then watch how that relationship changes over time.

Are you up to the challenge?

Totally yours

Nietzsche said man can be defined by his capacity to promise. One man who had remained faithful through many health challenges in his marriage, reflected on why he stuck with his family: "Sometimes I keep doing things because I love my family; sometimes I do things because it feels important to me personally. And sometimes I do things because *I promised.*"

Contrary to the view that love can be enjoyed in any circumstance, researcher Patricia Noller writes, "Commitment is very central to love - an important component of love is both the short-term and long-term commitment to the loved one and the relationship." In fact, she points out, "love does not seem possible without commitment." [42]

We're talking here about committing everything - with no conditions. This is the difference is between giving some, and giving all - between committing for awhile, versus committing for good - for always...as the phrase goes, "love me till my heart stops."

As Fromm summarized, "Love means to commit oneself without guarantee, to give oneself completely in the hope that our love will produce love in the loved person." [43] "Loyalty and commitment," Johnson points out, are "as necessary to us as food and air. Human beings have to be able to depend on each other....people can't really live out their love for one another in any meaningful way, unless human beings will truly honor the commitment they make to one another." [44]

Can you do that? Are you willing to go after it? I think you've got it in you! When it happens, this kind of total commitment sweeps away much of the tentativeness and hesitancy discussed earlier - with "ambiguity...resolved, and uncertainty...replaced by a certainty that acts do matter beyond their own time span." [45]

That kind of love, as one woman summarizes, "can offer a respite from perfectionism and performance anxieties. If you are truly loved, you can feel valued and cherished, no matter what happens at work. You are able to resist the constant pressure to compete, perform, and exceed expectations. You can have another life apart from your work life, where you are not subject to the same critical, judging, and evaluating scrutiny that you face every day in the workplace, or in the singles dating culture. [46]

This leads individuals to loving commitment through thick and thin, rather than only when the romantic feelings are cresting. This kind of constancy comes not from an unvarying feeling - but from a consistent practice of love.

More than simply a 'nice thing to try,' this commitment may be required of anyone seriously interested in lasting love. As Robert Johnson puts it, "a man is committed to a woman only when he can inwardly affirm that he binds himself to her as an individual and that he will be with her even when he is no longer 'in love,' even when he and she are no longer afire with passion and he no longer sees in her his ideal of perfection...When a man can say this inwardly, and mean it, then he has touched the essence of commitment." He then adds, by way of warning: "But he should know that he has an inner battle ahead of him."[47]

Leading your heart

If you're interested in pursuing a long-term relationships based on something deeper than immediate romance or passing affection, make no mistake: you will be challenged. The sheer force of past habits makes sure this path involves some major turbulence.

And for sure, none of this is as easy as it looks - not in a culture that relentlessly preaches the opposite: *Make sure you're Feeling Enough. Don't move forward without it!*

If you're interested in doing more than surviving this battle, then it's time to talk about the final skill you must master. We said earlier that you do not have to follow every thought that comes into your head. You don't have to yield to every feeling that comes into your heart. Instead, you can *watch* thoughts and feelings that arise...and decide what *you* want.

Rather than being dragged around by feelings that capture us, then leave - this is about a love that can be practiced and exercised. "You should not just follow your heart. You should *lead it*" Stephen and Alex Kendrick write: "Don't let your feelings and emotions do the driving. You put them in the back seat and tell them where you're going."[48]

This isn't about forcing yourself to do something you don't want - or trying to control and stifle your feelings. This is about being wise and skillful in how you relate to those feelings - and no longer being their slave.[49]

This is about standing up to a narrative of romance that invites us all to be slaves to our feelings. "We dare you to think differently" the Kendricks continue, and "choose to lead your heart toward that which is best in the long run. This is a key to lasting, fulfilling relationships."[50]

In a word, then, this view of feeling reinforces the basic capacity to direct one's own life. One woman who broke up four times with a man she cared about due to Not Feeling Enough, spoke of crying for many hours after breaking up once again. "I really wanted to date him and tried to feel what I thought I was *supposed to feel*, but the anticipated excitement kept going away so I thought that meant it wasn't right." Her father sat down with her and suggested she may have been misinterpreting these feelings:

> He told me that maybe I shouldn't be basing my decision on the intensity of my romantic feelings...but instead, the peace I feel about the relationship. I had never thought of peace as a way to tell if someone was a *good match* or not. I thought it was just all about the sparks. I realized that maybe the comfort and ease I felt around him was actually an indicator that he was a good person to date and I got really excited.

When she learned that there was another legitimate option, she felt an immediate release from the anxiety and quickly called up her ex-boyfriend. Upon her return, they started dating again and eventually got engaged.

As reflected here, the mere awareness of another way of approaching romantic feeling made a dramatic impact. By shifting from being driven by romantic feeling alone - to something deeper...something deeper than thought, and deeper than emotion - she felt able to actually make a choice and pursue the relationship further. Instead of driven by whatever the feeling-du-jour dictates, individuals may thus find some space and freedom that allows them to make conscious and deliberate choices in developing a relationship with an individual that seems especially well-suited to them. Rather than largely pursuing a particular *feeling*, individuals are thus empowered to legitimately pursue *a relationship*.

In this way, feeling comes to follow action. Instead of "I'm attracted to whom I'm attracted" - this suggests that our attractions change over time as we choose the direction we want to go.

This approach re-awakens individuals to become fully active participants in creating and cultivating love in their own relationships. Instead of largely waiting upon emotion as the primary mover and driver of relationships, we can re-direct attention towards caring for individuals around them.

And when challenges come, this kind of love perseveres and gives us the courage to say, 'I believe in this person and the potential of our relationship - and I'm not going to be bullied away from it. Deep and powerful assurances lead me on.'

In this way, decisions about relationships can be freed from the exclusive dominion of The Feeling. We become free to move forward at times (if we wish), despite vacillating feelings. On the wall of a concentration camp was written, "I believe in the sun when it is not shining. I believe in love even when I feel it not." Referring to initial feelings of excitement, one man said, "If we truly felt it is a good and healthy thing...we should remember what it felt like and do a 'wait and see'...continuing to date them." He added, "and in a marriage relationship...we say—'we felt this before and can feel it again.'"

So wherever you find yourself and your relationships: Keep your chin up! Keep your minds open! And let the deepest part of you and the whispers of peace do the guiding.

Chapter 10. Growing: Romance Alive

"True love stories never end."

During one of the darker and more confusing periods of my life, I attended an extended family party with my dear cousin, Natalie, who was also in her 30's and also unmarried. In the spaces between the laughter, the story sharing and the ice cream, there was easy enjoyment of being around people we loved, and whom we knew loved us.

As she and I carpooled back to our apartments and roommates, we relished the lingering aura of the event filled with an ease and abundance of loving. Reflecting on my years of heartbreaking romance, I blurted out to my cousin, "Why is it so dang hard to just love each other, Natalie? How could something that feels so natural and simple in other settings - be so impossible and confusing with those we are trying to date?!"

This is the question at the heart of this book: for something so incredibly sweet and wonderful as romantic love - how and why has it become such a brutal experience for so many?

You've now heard my answer to that question. As detailed in previous chapters, I believe what's behind much of the trouble is, simply put, a story: a particular narrative about love and romance - how they're supposed to be, how we're supposed to feel, etc.

Once we download and adopt that story, the machine starts to churn. Into that machine go our best hopes and, energy and our latest crush. Out the other side, with industrial-level efficiency, comes bitterness, fatigue and usually another break-up.

Heart-break after heart-break, this poisoning of relationships is depressingly predictable. Each time it happens, the despair, frustration and heartache only grow.

This is the heartache that pushed me to these questions: Is there another way to do this? Another way to think about it? Another story to live out?

In a hundred different ways, through hundreds of different voices and experiences, the answer screaming back to me was YES! You bet. *Absolutely.*

There's more than one story of romance to follow. As you've seen yourself, there's another narrative out there - a lovely story - and one with beautiful consequences. This potentially includes more freedom, more stability and more enjoyment in our romance - each the subject of prior chapters.

While all that sounds all nice and good in theory, however, what about those of us who are so tired and worn out from all the drama that we're just...not feeling it? Apathy. Not interested. Done (see Chapter 5).

Are you really asking us to try again? To put ourselves out there and expect anything different?

The answer is yes. You deserve something different. And it's time to get on it.

The great surprise

My college roommate, Trevor, dated a girl his senior year that he liked. He wouldn't say he was 'in love' with her - but they connected in many ways and they felt their love growing. I stayed up with him till midnight one night while he tried to decide whether to propose to her..."Do I love her enough?" Unlike many, many stories I have heard, he decided to go for it. They got married 7 years ago, and have had 4 children.

I saw him at a get-together recently. I asked him, 'Trevor, would you say you were in love when you got married?' He waxed philosophical, saying, "What does 'being in love' really mean, Jacob?" Thinking of his wife now, I asked him, "Well what about now? Would you say you and your wife are in love now?" "Ahhh, yes," he quickly responded: "*Oh, yeah.* Definitely," with a broad smile.

And that's the big surprise. Simply put, love - true love - grows...even where you don't expect it. Affection and attraction, given the right match, also grows. "With my fiancé," he said, "initially, I wouldn't have picked her out of a crowd...at first glance, she didn't register." "But now," he added with some amazement, "there are very few that I would consider more attractive....the physical attraction I feel with her is just growing."

As described earlier, one woman was not only not attracted to her husband upon first meeting, she thought he looked like a cancer patient. Although his physical appearance hadn't changed, the more she talkd with him, many other things about him began to stand out: his personality, sense of humor, etc. Interestingly enough, all of this started to "make him" very attractive to her - not just emotionally or intellectually, but *physically*! "I started to notice his eyes - his smile started to stand out, " she said. "To this day, I consider him one of the most attractive men I have met."

Wow! Physical attraction spurred by a deeper sense of someone's worth. Pretty cool stuff. Another woman recounted, "I didn't even like my husband when I met him. I was working in fashion and he was schlubby....sort of an oddball. He asked me out and I didn't want to go out with him. But he was persistent and as I got to know him, he not only turned out to be a wonderful guy, but he turned out to be the love of my life."[1] A third person said, "When you see a person's soul, he or she can become more attractive to you."

But isn't love Supposed To Arise dramatically, quickly - even spontaneously? Not only can this expectation feel too rigid - it also does not map onto the love experiences many couples end up finding. I asked one friend at his wedding reception, "Wo would you say that you two fell in love?" He admitted, "That's not really what happened...it's more like we *grew in love*." Instead of 'falling into' their romance, a surprising number of couples experience a slower, more gradual, and budding process of love development: something that may emerge more naturally.

Cultivating desire

This isn't something we typically expect - or even plan on. But it's absolutely reliable as a relationship pathway. One researcher proposed romantic love be re-framed as "an attachment process" - a gradually developing "biosocial process by which affectional bonds are formed between adult lovers, just as affectional bonds are formed earlier in life between human infants and their parents."[2]

Regarding their happy marriage and its pre-arrangement by parents, one couple from India was asked, "How did you know you would love her? Did you ever worry that you weren't going to love each other?" The man responded, "I didn't get that thought. I don't personally believe that love just happens to you [but is instead] the byproduct" of other decisions. He explained, "We're not forced to love; we love each other. because of our marriage." Instead of having to feel something particular prior to committing, he explained, it's also possible that all the feelings and love can "grow out of" such a total commitment.

Rather than finding the one and absolute best individual for us, this is about moving towards an amazing relationship with a person good for us. This is about ensuring, as one author put it, "a particular type of environment in which both the lovers and those dependent on them can grow and develop."[3] As a result, we can anticipate a growing love over time - call it, *becoming soul mates?*

Like growing any living thing, this kind of cultivation requires significant patience. Indeed, a relationship's true potential may not even be evident for awhile, with time sometimes needed "to sow, cultivate and feed desire." As Bauman elaborates, "Desire needs time to germinate, grow and mellow."[4] Quentin Crisp suggests that loving another person requires us to "undertake some fragment of their destiny." From this view, love is something grasped in pieces and imperfectly initially - anticipating a fuller understanding and expression after long development over time. Bauman adds, "It is not in craving after ready-made, complete and finished things that love finds its meaning - but in the urge to participate in the becoming of such things."[5]

"We don't expect to be growing further in love," one person commented - admitting it is very hard to be open to that sort of development in a relationship. Indeed, while there are literally thousands of cultural depictions of intense, passionate don't-stop-kissing-me-or-I-die-now relationships, there are admittedly far fewer examples of a more gradual unfolding. One woman notes, "Books seem to have more time for a relationship to progress than movies do. Perhaps that is why Hollywood has the whirlwind romance thing going on – they don't have time to develop anything more."

There are, of course, some exceptions. One novel-made-into-a-film depicts love that "comes softly"[6] - rather than suddenly and overwhelmingly. And the award-winning *The Painted Veil* is one of the most authentic visions of this shifting, evolving beauty of love I've ever seen.[7] Through the character Anne (of Green Gables), Montgomery writes, "Perhaps, after all, romance did not come into one's life with pomp and blare, like a gay knight riding down; perhaps it crept to one's side like an old friend through quiet ways."[8]

Commitment may thus be seriously considered even before flaming passion arrives - an idea that seems odd within Western culture, if not others. One Asian author paraphrases a saying from his country: "In the West, marriage is like a boiling teakettle that is taken off the stove. It starts off hot but soon turns cold. In the East, marriage is like a dish that is placed on a hotplate. It begins cold but gradually warms up."[9]

It would be nice, of course, if this kind of moving forward was always accompanied by a constant and linear growth in passionate love. While this may be the case for some, for many others the level of feeling can ebb and flow, sometimes shifting in fits and starts. But as you commit to someone - the point is this: initially and over time - your heart and mind can start to grow in true, deeper love. As one woman said, "They said they always felt peace from the beginning, just not the roller coaster ride giddiness so often portrayed in the movies. However, as they allowed the relationship to progress over time, the love did too."

In a number of ways, then, we can cultivate a heightened capacity to love - alongside an expanded vision of who even qualifies as 'loveable.' The bottom line is this: Believe that relationships grow! As individuals continue to invest in relationships where they do not necessarily feel overwhelming passion - but with whom they *do* connect in substantial ways - they may be surprised what they find.

Sticking with it

One man who previously struggled to pursue girls unless he was "completely blown away" described graduating from college with things still not working out socially. He then recounted a major turning point in his approach to love life: "A friend sat me down and gave me some pretty good advice, 'you need to be in a relationship, even if it doesn't work, even if you aren't twitter pated, even if she is not the most attractive person [you've ever met]. You need to commit that 'I'm going to date this girl and have a really meaningful relationship and see where this goes.'" He continued, "I realized as long as they are within a certain range of attractiveness, you should just go for it - rather than waiting for some magic that is going to come around." The man said that this advice "totally changed my perception of what it meant to date." He explained, "[once you really commit, your brain starts to move towards this person in a way that it doesn't before you do that. I was amazed at how my feelings started to evolve with that...What it taught me was how much your feelings can evolve when you commit."

As we commit to really sticking with relationships - we can begin to see much more clearly who is well suited (or not) to our personality and interests. This same man above described what happened next:

From there, I dated just a handful more girls. With each one, I kind of experienced the same thing: As you commit and really get to know someone, you see who that person is. And in every case, I saw she wouldn't be a *good match* (which I wouldn't have known based on my initial feelings of excitement). Time and time again I thought I had found someone - it was pretty frustrating. But I did it right: dating her long enough to know if it would progress, [before] ending it. Never the hot and cold thing - instead, hanging in there long enough until I was absolutely sure I knew she was not a person I could marry.

He was then introduced to another person. "When I first saw my wife, I thought she was attractive, but she looked so much like my mother at that age." Nonetheless, he continued, "I could tell she was smart and informed. Again, I was not overly attracted, but I could tell she was quality and made the decision, 'I'm going to spend time with her.'" He finished the story, "When I did, the more I was around her, the more I liked her. She had the same goals as I did, and I fell in love with her family. Pretty quickly, I was able to take each step; now we're in wedding planning mode. I found the match for me."

Rather than rapidly concluding that someone is "just not my type," this is about giving people and our relationships with them a bit more patience: "right off the bat, the person may not get a favorable impression, but everyone deserves a second chance." We become more willing to be open and try things out, without first being head over heels as a prerequisite condition.

Sticking with a relationship means you give it a chance - even when things aren't ideal. If you believe love and attraction always happen immediately, of course, then sticking with a relationship makes little sense. Rather than specifying a limited amount of time for a state to be felt, relationships may thus be given some time to develop. As one interview participant said, "I wish I would see people dating for longer periods of time, instead of ending the relationship because you just aren't 'feeling it'...it limits how much people can actually get to know each other, because they are waiting for that magic something, and they don't really have enough time to get past the awkward period to really get to know each other."

At some point, clearly it may be time to let go after time proves attraction only diminishing. One woman spoke of people "I first thought someone was attractive - 'wow' - and as I got to know them and talked with them, this declined."

When deciding to move away from someone, it's not a choice we make impulsively. Nor are we as inclined to break up solely because the current feeling is not-exciting-enough. While breaking up may, in fact, be the right decision - it's *our decision* - not simply a result of whatever feeling is present. And it's a decision we can make with a level of mindfulness and care.

One man felt anxious and awkward after dates, as "I spent a lot of time...dissecting what had happened" - until, he thought more about other relationships - including friendships with guy friends. Reflecting on these male friends, he remarked "there was no magic moment or explosion for the relationship to materialize. I just happened to be in a random circumstance and happened to be talking to these guys - and it turned into a really great relationship." He continued, "I never sat down with my best friend and said, "Look, we've played Frisbee two times; I'm feeling something, and think we should take this somewhere.'...I never went to an activity with a guy friend and said, 'I'm through...I'm done with you...I've reviewed our recent activities and it's over.'...We never had these super-detailed, over-the-top analyses with all these people I loved...it was just being a kind, friendly person to anyone who crossed your path. A lot of these people you just happen to run into blossomed into fantastic friends."

His wife described just getting out of a relationship of "manipulation and game-playing" - and how "refreshing it was to have it be so natural." What would it be like if dating were actually like other kinds of relationships? Non-strategic...non-agenda...no special rules....treating everyone with love - no matter whether they are a possibility.

When you do find a relationship drawing you in, your initial work is simply this: doing your best to hold your expectations gently, *practicing openness, and curiosity. Rather than just hard work in a relationship - this is about* heart work: *ensuring your own heart and mind are fully open to the face in front of you.*

Among other things, this can help us avoid starting or ending relationships so quickly. When we give them some time, they may surprise us. One man admitted, "There are many girls I have taken on dates that I have gotten along with great, but as far as keeping the relationship going, I had no interest....I would get bored." After many years of such break-ups, this man spoke of making a change with a recent relationship: "She was the first girl I actually stuck with, and I surprised myself by becoming more and more excited about the relationship and attracted to her as the relationship progressed, despite the lack of a strong initial spark."

Unhappily ever after?

When you're in the middle of a challenging relationship, all this can sound like a bunch of hogwash: you're encouraging me to do what?

Stick with it. That's what! But let's be clear - this isn't about resigning yourself in a painful relationship. Research at UCLA has shown that couples who stayed committed during times of stress were more likely to be happier (and together) later on.[10]

Even difficult relationships tend to improve and become stronger over time - much stronger. It gets better! One recent large-scale study indicates that 86% of people who said they were unhappily married in the late 1980s but stayed married, indicated that they were happier when interviewed five years later. Indeed, three-fifths of the formerly unhappily married couples rated their marriages as either "very happy" or "quite happy."[11]

Walking away takes no personal growth and no effort, other than walking itself. This is about taking a braver, gutsier option - one that calls on everything you've got. As one author proposes, "The disintegration of romantic love is not a tragic loss. Rather, it is the beginning of the possibility of real growth within you."[12]

Becoming an artist

Rather than reflecting a momentary commitment, the kind of change undergirding this kind of love calls for deep and sustained attention. In this sense, Fromm speaks of love as an *art* to be developed and refined over time: "If one wants to become a master in any art, one's whole life must be devoted to it, or at least related to it. One's own person becomes an instrument in the practice of the art." This means, he explains, that:

One must learn a great number of other - and often seemingly disconnected - things before one starts with the art itself. With regard to the art of loving, this means that anyone who aspires to become a master in this art must begin by practicing discipline, concentration and patience throughout every phase of his life. The capacity to love demands a state of intensity, awareness, enhanced vitality, which can only be the result of a productive and active orientation in many other spheres of life.[13]

The provocative idea here is that the capacity to love does not stand-alone, but instead depends on other qualities and attributes. This idea stands in stark contrast to common assumptions discussed earlier - namely, that love is something anyone can experience: just come across the right person, at the right moment, stoke the right emotions - and viola!

While it's true that such infatuation is almost a universal experience, deeper, more lasting kinds of love, may need something unique. The suggestion here is somewhat remarkable: In order to love another human being fully and completely, we need to become a *certain kind of person*!

That's some tough medicine. Wouldn't it be so nice to believe that we could act however we want - and *still* experience all the satisfying love we want? On this point, Fromm warns, "It is an illusion to believe that one can separate life in such a way that one is productive in the sphere of love and unproductive in all other spheres."[14]

From confronting family-of-origin issues to lifestyle habits getting in the way of empathy, in order to practice love in this way, a personal change may be necessary. "Transformation," one author writes, "is the one solution to the conflicts, the confused loyalties, and the terrible sufferings of romance. The only true resolution is a change of consciousness."[15] In this way, we may come to see our romantic relationships as opportunities for growth in our capacity to love and be committed to another human being.[16]

This is different than saying singles are messed up or broken. Instead of needing to be fixed, we simply need restoration. In place of correcting internal deficiency, this is about stopping our resisting of who we most deeply are.

Over time, this kind of effort can lead to wonderful shifts. One man who spoke of his struggles to feel love for others, said, "My ability to show love is like a little sapling, never given the nurture it needed - a few branches, leaves and acorns." The good news, he added, is that "You can grow that tree. That's my job is to be able to grow that, and be able to love and give love. For other people, their tree is bigger and they have more capacity to love." He went on to describe how the way one lives their life "will increase [their] capacity to love" - hinting that if he had lived differently, "[he] would have loved more."

He concluded, "Learning to love takes care of so many issues. Why don't we love? That is complex. The need to love...is not."

For those unwilling to make changes, then, love can become a near impossibility. Describing her experience with a former boyfriend, one woman recounted, "He wanted to have a spouse and family, but he just wasn't willing or didn't know how to do the work to take care of his issues getting in the way. If he was really serious about finding answers, they were there." She recollected thinking, "I'm a person he could really connect with...but it wasn't enough for him." When she encouraged him to move in that direction, "he bolted...he just ran away - stopped calling, stopped communicating."

Restoring dating culture

What about those of us who *don't* want to run away anymore - those reformed-bolters (such as myself) - who are eager to move decisively in another direction?

Rather than trying to run the whole race at once - it may be good if we started with a few baby steps. How about some high quality dates for starters?

As we saw earlier, many have concluded that dating culture has become "obsolete"[17] or even dead - with no going back! Many of these same authors, however, would be quick to advocate for saving nearly-extinct wildlife or working hard to preserve wetlands, forests, old buildings and other things of value.

Why not show the same kind of persistence and perseverance in restoring and re-enshrining another natural resource that we've almost lost: "the date" as a valuable social encounter? As one person said, "Going out to dinner is what you do with people who are important to you. It is what you do when your parents come to visit, when you meet a business partner, when you celebrate friendships. Why not as a way to begin a potential relationship?" Speaking of her own relationship she continued, "We never once went out early on in our relationship without making it a formal date, because we both felt that was a respectful way to treat someone you may want to establish an important relationship with. If a person can't treat a dating relationship with respect, would he treat a marriage so? Would he keep family dinners or extended family gatherings on Sundays?" [18]

One person admits, "In today's hangout culture it takes courage to ask for dates, to continue in the process even after rejection and failure, and to commit to one person in the face of so many wonderful people."

Let's give it a shot! And if you approach this next date or your current relationship from the broader, more generous and gentle mindset discussed above, I can promise you one thing: your love life will stop hurting so much.

And who knows? Relationships may even start to be enjoya-ble. And when you meet someone who's a Good Match for you, maybe you will be more likely to recognize him or her - for who they really are.

If and when you decide that you don't Feel Enough, you may opt to continue exploring that relationship anyway. Can you see where this might be leading?

The degree to which you plunge in and immerse yourself in this 'counter-cultural' narrative of love we've been exploring, you will be much closer to taking the real plunge and making the radical move called total commitment.

The M word

Anyone living in our current society must be careful about using either of the "M" words. One woman said "I always wanted to be a mother, but I never tell men that's what I want because I'm afraid they'd leave me." [19] "Marriage" is also a word that we "use timidly, or ironically, perhaps," one author notes, because we've "been warned that talk of marriage can seem needy or desperate."[20]

The larger culture can reinforce this in its "lack of social sympathy" for a person's interest in marriage. One author writes, "Women are *supposed to* stand on their own two feet, not feel weak in the knees; they're supposed to enjoy sex for fun, not whine about commitment...if they express a desire for marriage, they've somehow violated the social compact." She goes on to ask, "when did the search for someone to marry become self-absorbed and pathetic?"[21]

Rather than something obsolete or outdated, "according to virtually every poll and survey conducted on the subject," summarizes one research report, "the vast majority of young women say they want to be married someday." The men aren't far behind - with 80 percent of young-adult men and women continuing to report marriage as an "important" part of their life plan.[22]

This certainly isn't true of everyone - with many holding fundamental, even damning questions about marriage. A substantial majority (88%) agree that it is more difficult to have a good marriage today than in their parents' generation, and slightly more than half (52%) agree that one sees so few good or happy marriages that one questions it as a way of life.[23] "Divorce was to Gen-X what Vietnam was to the Baby Boom," writes Barbara Whitehead. "It shaped the outlook of an entire generation...it conveyed one indelible lesson: namely, that marriage is unreliable as an economic partnership and precarious as a life vocation...Far from being a safe bet...marriage is a gamble."[24]

'All right' some might say - it's okay to go ahead and get married. *Just make sure to not do it too early!*' A strong cultural message has cropped up over recent decades that getting married earlier is a patently bad idea and leads to patently bad results.

Statistical research, however, tells a very different story - with "sharp benefits and few disadvantages to marrying in the 20s." In fact, "women who were married in their 20s are more likely to call themselves 'very happy' in marriage." One recent study by sociologists Norval Glenn and Jeremy Uecker examined five different large data sets and concluded that "the greatest indicated likelihood of being in an intact marriage of the highest quality is among those who married at ages 22-25."[25]

Compared to married twentysomethings, unmarried twentysomethings are significantly more likely to drink to excess, to be depressed, and to report lower levels of satisfaction with their lives. The advantage holds over cohabiting friends as well. Only 35 percent of single men and cohabiting men report they are "highly satisfied" with their life, compared to 52 percent of married men. Likewise, 33 percent of single women and 29 percent of cohabiting women are "highly satisfied," compared to 47 percent of married women. when they marry in their midtwenties.[26] Fertility also peaks around age 28.[27] Twenty percent of women older than 40 are childless - up 80% since 1976.[28]

One author writes, "Most women are living with the fantasy that they can behave exactly like men in their twenties and then sometime in their thirties, when they're ready, they'll find a comfy, stable dude to settle down with who'll be a big provider. They think this while they're training men to do the exact opposite." Many people are now saying, for instance, "It's too early. I want to just have fun in my twenties." She continues, "This is one of the most dangerous narratives for women who eventually want a committed relationship and /or motherhood....not only are we training ourselves for frequent short-term, low-criteria relationships...we are training men for long-term bachelorhood."[29]

"The best boyfriend I ever had was when I was in my mid-twenties" one woman in her 30s said, "I just didn't think I was *supposed to be* [married] with someone then."[30] This author concludes, "The broader culture should respect the choice of twentysomethings to marry...provided that they are in a good relationship." So, for twentysomethings in a good relationship, marriage is an option that should not be ignored or devalued." Families, friends and the larger culture "should encourage today's twentysomethings to weave together their plans for parenthood and marriage and to align those plans with their sexual behavior."[31]

Why not celebrate and encourage two individuals willing to make this kind of total commitment? There is a beauty of its own in any enduring, faithful companionship.

Lori Gottlieb proposes that in our current culture "the idea of choosing to run a household together - as unglamorous and challenging and mundane" as that is - reflects the ultimate act of 'true love.'"[32]

Commit

There is something gutsy about such an act - about going against all the you-are-depriving-yourself propaganda (e.g., 'She's good enough for you, etc.') - and coming to a decisive response in a relationship: 'Hey, this *is* what I want. And you know what? It's *even better* than what the culture tells me I *should want.*

> *I like to throw out this fun litmus test to single friends as a quick self-assessment: Can you name 5 individuals right now that you could be happy with as your life-long partner? For a surprising number of people, their answer is, "None that I can think of?" If that's your answer, you might want to do some serious thinking about the questions we've explored in this book. Wherever you find yourself, know this: A good sign of someone ready for a lasting romance is this: They see LOTS of amazing, beautiful people around them. Do you?*

If you haven't yet, starting today begin peeling back the cultural narrative from your face, like a bad mask. Then look around: What do you see? Are you ready to embrace another human being - for real?

Nobody's saying to go out and commit to just anyone. Instead, this is about perhaps reviving some of your flagging faith that it is possible to find lasting love and reassuring you that it may not be as hard as we often make it out to be!

When the next right person comes around - will you be ready?

Conclusion

"A little rebellion is a good thing."
- Thomas Jefferson

Once upon a time, a relationship started that seemed just right. Over time as this couple got to know each other more, the connection deepened and they started talking about a life together.

There was one problem: for both of them, their feelings were not always glorious or passionate or intense. They had sweet moments of excitement, for sure. Most of the time, however, emotions cruised along pretty normal - without special fireworks.

Despite this, after searching their hearts and feeling some peace about their future, they decided on a life together.

And they were eventually married.

And they stayed married...through better and worse.

And they were happy. The end.

Hold on, now! Where is the part of the story about her being drop-dead gorgeous? Or the irrational crazy levels of passion? What about the months of excruciating back and forth as they decide whether they like each other enough to cut-off-all-other-options?

Surely we've been taught better than this. We all know that relationships can't go that smooth nowadays, right?

Proselyting delusion

In the final years of writing this book, the Syrian people have been pursuing a revolution for freedom. It's been hard to understand how non-violent protesters could be called 'armed thugs' or 'dangerous terrorists' by the Syrian government. Such profound misrepresentation of reality felt strange and completely foreign to my experience.

Then I wrote this book. Studying the discourse around love, beauty and relationships has shaken me and opened my eyes. Although nothing quite compares to the gross distortions of the Syrian News Agency, it's important to realize we face our own very real and influential propaganda in other areas: *'You deserve better...your partner should look like this...your feelings Should Be more exhilirating than this...come on - you deserve better!'*

It's not by sheer chance that we've become vulnerable to this kind of "mindweather." Neither is it because these rapid-fire thoughts are 'natural' to love.

Thanks to multi-billion dollar budgets, we're exposed to over **1500** marketing pitches in an average week[1] alongside many additional hours of other kinds of screen time - much of which involves some kind of romance.

There is more than entertainment going on, of course. There is teaching. And listening. And learning.

The literalness with which the dominant story of romance is taken for granted in our current society is nothing short of remarkable. You know when a story or way of thinking has become truly powerful, when it *ceases* to be seen as a story.

The dominant story-line has so effectively flipped our romantic world upside down, that we end up feeling *trapped* by the very relationships that are good for us and repelled by the very individuals who could make our lives more beautiful. At the same time, of course, we're often equally persuaded to go after relationships that give us very little of what we need (and really want) over the long-term.

No more

Why does all this matter, again? Because every day, an amazing man walks away from an equally amazing woman...not because either of them are not worth it.

Not by a lack of effort, or lack of intelligence or lack of anything personal in particular - but because they've been hijacked - by an incessant, daily download from the surrounding culture regarding how it's Supposed To Be, how you're Supposed To Look, and how you're Supposed To Feel.

I'm tired of seeing wonderful couples messed with: good men and women being duped into walking away from beautiful relationships en masse - not because the other person is not *wonderful,* not because the other person's not a Good Fit - but because they've been convinced the connection, the attraction, the passion and the person is *not wonderful enough.*

In my own life, an exciting realization finally settled on my soul: *I don't have to do this anymore.* I don't have to be driven away from an amazing person just because my feeling settles a little. I don't have to be mesmerized by a narrow, fun-house-mirror version of beauty - to the point that I no longer see and appreciate the person in front of me.

If you're also tired of status quo romance, you know by now that there's something you and I can do.

We can rebel. We can defy and disobey the shrunken relationship standards of the culture around us - and choose to lead our hearts in another direction.

Romance, the revolution

Like happened with the "Truth Campaign" against Big Tobacco, it's past time for a Truth campaign directed at the cultural forces toxic to intimate relationships.

One treatment center in San Francisco that specializes in eating disorders built an entire program around helping girls resist anorexia and bulimia by helping to "surface" and publically "unmask" the cultural "voice of eating disorders." By identifying and externalizing the propaganda or rhetoric that fuel eating disorders, they found these ideas losing their power and grip over girls since they are no longer seen as Reality itself.[2]

I write this book in hopes of contributing to similar efforts to surface and "unmask" the different cultural voices, rhetoric and propaganda at play in American love - messages that are driving our relationships into the ground[3] as they beat upon us, one again: *'You Deserve Better...you don't Feel Enough...this person is Not Enough...you Deserve Better!!'*

What if you don't deserve better? What if the feeling in your relationship is enough? What if this partner you're with is *more than enough* and would, in fact, be an incredible partner for you?

As long as our attention is monopolized by one far reaching story, of course, these kinds of possibilities are not even on the table. Instead, the terms of our relationships are set by a loud and convincing culture. As long as we have no grasp of another viable story, it remains difficult to think and act for ourselves.[4]

As a result, our sense of freedom in relationships can become extremely limited. If McDonalds is the only place in town, we all eat Big Macs. But as options are introduced, suddenly a discussion begins. And choices are on the table.

Re-storying love

This book is not about presenting a new-fangled story of romance. Neither is it about condemning everything we usually believe about love. Instead, the aim is to pay more serious attention to whatever story we decide to hold onto - and what it means for our real life.

In the words of one author, to better understand love, we need to "demythologize" common narratives, listening between the lines until we figure out the fictional, the factual and the some-where-in-between.[5] Taking a cue from Eastern, contemplative traditions, Robert Johnson writes, we can learn to "stand outside ourselves, outside our assumptions and our beliefs, just long enough to see ourselves in a new perspective. We can learn what it is to approach love with a different set of attitudes, unburdened by the dogmas of our culture."

This entails a different scientific project than attempting to 'figure out the factors' that purportedly explain love. Instead, the aim of such a narrative research project is 'map out' the existing narratives of romance in as systematic and rigorous a way as possible. Like a good cartographer, I've tried to chart out the territory as I'm seeing it: figuring out key divides, crucial water-ways and contested areas of the landscape.

Within a discourse in which the very meaning of love has been profoundly confused, increased clarity around simple distinctions may alone be helpful. As Scott Peck stated:

Our use of the word "love" is so generalized and unspecific as to severely interfere with our understanding of love. As long as we continue to use the word "love" to describe our relationship with anything that is important to us...without regard for the quality of that relationship, we will continue to have difficulty.[6]

Johnson similarly added that people "use the phase 'romantic love' indiscriminately to refer to almost any attraction":

We use the term for many things that are not romantic love at all. We assume that if it is love, it must be 'romance,' and if it is romance, it must be 'love'.... we have lost the consciousness of what love is, what romance is, and what the differences are between them. We are confusing two great [dynamics] within us, and this has a devastating effect on our lives and our relationships.[7]

Awareness itself then, can spur changes. By unsettling the dominant narrative about The Way Things Are, we may then actually unsettle *the way things are.*

Whether or not we pay attention to these different ways of thinking, however, mark my words: they will exert their influence. Especially when acting beneath our awareness, Johnson continues, certain ways of thinking can "absolutely possess us and dominate us from the depths."[8]

This is about becoming free from a kind of slavery to assumptions and expectations we may not even know we're making. In turn, we can consider possibilities that are no longer unthinkable. As Lori Gottlieb writes, one "distinguishing quality" of those singles who find lasting romance in committed relationships is their ability to "redefine romance."[9]

It's easy to confuse what I'm saying. After reading the book, one woman said "So, I guess that means that we can't believe in fairytales – not the ones about love anyway. Where does that leave Disney and Cinderella?? You might not be on their list of favorite people."

To be absolutely clear, the *last thing* I want to do is undercut dreams and aspirations. Rather than trying to crush any sweet hopes of romance, this is about better protecting and securing these possibilities against forces that *will* crush them.

Broadening the conversation

Why again so much focus on interpretation, narrative and story? According to one tradition of continental philosophy, what differentiates between very different life experiences are the different interpretations and ways of thinking that undergird them. In other words, we don't just 'tell' stories and narratives - we *live them out.*[10]

Why are increasing numbers of people unable to experience lasting love? You've heard a hundred answers from family parties to magazine articles. And now you've heard mine: because of the story we've downloaded and adopted. Period.

As detailed throughout the book, competing narratives of romance may lead people in very different directions. Regardless of whether the individual actors are conscious of it happening, the differing 'scripts' in their head manifest in profoundly different ways of acting, dating, relating, kissing, loving, breaking up, etc.

Getting clear about interpretation, then, has *everything* to do with the quality and staying-power of the love and romance in our lives. More than in our status or situation, we are stuck in a story.

These stories can be powerful enough to override deeper intuitions and senses - prompting individuals to act contrary to their better intentions. In multiple ways, then, these bruising narratives can leave their mark. People are hurt who didn't deserve to be hurt. Relationships are damaged that had a beautiful future.

I have lived the very life that I decry. In my own painful experience, I look back and see how blind (and blinded) I have been - with lies colonizing my mind and heart in the very moment when I most needed clarity.

The good news is this: As narratives change fundamentally, practice follows. That means - things can change! In fact, as individuals conform to a particular mindset, their very brain and body begin to confirm it. Our actions, in turn, can begin to shape our story in reverse.

No matter what happend in the past, this is a new moment. And it's up to us what that moment looks like.

Let's be clear, though: If we believe the world's ideas about love and relationships simply are 'just a little off,' then our adjustments to practice will also be slight: adding a few new techniques to our dating style or polishing up our communication somehow. If the larger culture is *way off*, however, then something more may be necessary.

A new counterculture?

As hinted in the latter half of the book, a counter-culture is already on the rise. Instead of attempting to fix or correct individuals' thoughts or attitudes, this culture's invitation is simply to let go of one set of ideas and practices - and to embrace another.

Rather than playing endless defense maneuvers with the larger culture, maybe it's time to go on the offensive. Other authors have insinuated strongly that revolution is in the air.[11] This counter-insurgency would be made up of individuals like ourselves who feel ready for something more.

One of my hopes in writing this book is to inspire resistance to the rhetoric that supports and sustains current relationship patterns. As we become aware of our socialization within dominant narratives, may we thus discover how to potentially neutralize and opt out of continued socialization. By sharing "transgressive text" on websites, blogs and social media, we can all incite resistance and rebellion.[12] In the months ahead, I aim to gather and catalogue readers' experiences, stories and insights on my own website (see www.notfeelingit.org).

As we talk about these patterns in the light of day, we can perhaps release ourselves from their grip. Though we cannot directly affect the images in media, Naomi Wolff writes, "we can drain them of their power. We can turn away from them and look directly at one another" - lifting ourselves out of the myth.[13] In this way, we can - in the words of the poet Kabir - "let go of all thoughts of imaginary things."

While the larger changes continue to evolve, we can thus work to create our own 'micro-culture' that promotes, fosters and cultivates relational health. If individual couples and families cannot change the whole world (right away), at least we can create a healthy atmosphere for those closest to us. As we do so, we can then collectively spark and strengthen a more concerted movement of *true beauty* and *true love*.

While larger societal changes will take time, research has shown that one single voice raising questions in a group - especially if that voice is determined, consistent and clear enough - can sway the rest of the members.[14] Why not try?

One day more

For those open to the possibilities discussed in this book, a real-life adventure lies ahead. "For both men and women," Johnson writes, "to look honestly at romantic love is a heroic journey" - forcing us to look "at the contradictions and illusions we carry around inside us" and being willing to move through the "dark valleys and difficult confrontations" that heroic journeys always require.[15]

So who's up for an adventure? "Don't give up and don't get discouraged" Kendrick writes: "Resolve to lead your heart and to make it through to the end. *Learning to truly love is one of the most important things you will ever do.*"[16]

Do you believe that? If it's true, then loving another person completely may take everything we've got.

Let's stop walking away from people who are Good Matches. Let's stop saddling our love lives with manufactured stories of how things are Supposed To Be. And let's refuse to give up our hearts to imaginary things. In all these ways, let's stop allowing the culture to set the terms for our relationships - and decide to do it differently.

Let's start seeing people as they are - and let each other be human. Let's start leading our hearts, rather than being dragged around by our feelings. Let's pay attention to beauty that is bigger and deeper than anything the culture relishes - and start setting our sights on a truly whole-souled romance. Let's find someone who is a Good Match - a legitimate fit - and really commit to trying out the relationship. Let's follow the peace in this process, especially during the turbulence.

Bottom line: let's embrace this bigger, sweeter story of romance, and follow it all the way to our own real-life happy endings.

No matter what happened yesterday, no matter what the chatter around us says, this is a new moment - with a new story.

I'm rooting for you!

About the Author

After graduating as the psychology department valedictorian as an undergraduate, Jacob Hess studied in the clinical-community psychology doctoral program at the University of Illinois, Urbana-Champaign. While there, he was invited by the UIUC Program on Intergroup Relations to help develop and co-facilitate a liberal-conservative dialogue class for undergraduates, the first of its kind in the nation. Jacob's dissertation research explored competing narratives of depression and its medical treatment.

After finishing his Ph.D., Jacob worked as Research Director at a charity for abused children for three years, where he conducted long-term treatment outcome studies. More recently, with mindfulness teacher Thomas McConkie, Jacob co-founded a new non-profit, *All of Life* (www.alloflife.org), focused on developing risk-factor based mental health education.

Over the last couple of years, Jacob has published 12 peer-reviewed articles and recently co-authored a book on liberal-conservative dialogue with Dr. Phil Neisser (State University of New York, Potsdam), entitled, *You're Not as Crazy as I Thought (But You're Still Wrong)* – recently featured on NPR's *This American Life*. Jacob has also worked closely with *Fight the New Drug* (www.fightthenewdrug.org) in the development of their new online program, *Fortify*, for those facing pornography addiction.

Jacob is married to Monique Moore - with two little boys - William and Sammy - who make their daddy smile at least 9 times a day.

Notes

Preface

[1] Barbara Dafoe Whitehead, Why There Are No Good Men Left: The Romantic Plight of the New Single Woman (New York: Broadway Books, 2003), 2, 19, 188.

Introduction

[1] M. E. Scott, et al. "Young Adults Attitudes About Relationships and Marriage: Times May Have Changed, But Expectations Remain High," Child Trends Research Brief, Publication #2009-30, 4-5. (2009).

[2] Peggy Fletcher Stack, "Why Young LDS Men are Pushing Back Marriage" The Salt Lake Tribune (2011, April 19).

[3] Leigh Dethman and Nicole Warburton, "LDS and Single." Deseret Morning News. (2007, Mar 31).

[4] Kay Hymowitz, Jason S. Carroll, W. Bradford Wilcox and Kelleen Kaye, "Knot Yet: The Benefits and Costs of Delayed Marriage in America," National Marriage Project at the University of Virginia (2013).

[5] Karin Anderson, "Still single? What's the matter with you?" Special to CNN, (2010, August 13). [Author of "It Just Hasn't Happened Yet." Clifton Hills Press (2010)]

[6] Barbara Dafoe Whitehead, Why There Are No Good Men Left: The Romantic Plight of the New Single Woman (New York: Broadway Books, 2003), 8.

[7] Karin Anderson, "Still single? What's the matter with you?" Special to CNN, (2010, August 13). [Author of "It Just Hasn't Happened Yet." Clifton Hills Press (2010)]

[8] Mark Williams and colleagues writes, "What if there is nothing wrong. at all? What if. you have become a victim of your own very sensible, even heroic, efforts. like someone pulled even deeper into quicksand by the struggling intended to get you out?" (The Mindful Way Through Depression, 2007, 1-2).

[9] http://notfeelingit.org

[10] M. E. Addis and C.R. Martell, (2004). Overcoming depression one step at a time: The new behavioral activation approach to getting your life back. Oakland, CA: New Harbinger Publications.

[11] Naomi Wolf, The Beauty Myth: How Images of Beauty are Used Against Women (New York: Harper Perennial, 1992/2002), 162.

[12] American Psychological Association, Task Force on the Sexualization of Girls. (2010). Report of the APA Task Force on the Sexualization of Girls.

[13] Deborah Schooler and L. Monique Ward "Average Joes: Men's relationships with media, real bodies, and sexuality." *Psychology of Men & Masculinity,* 7(1), 27–41 (2006).

[14] Ian *Kerner,* "How porn is changing our sex lives." *CNN (2011, Jan 20).*

[15] Susie Orbach, *Bodies* (Bodies. New York: Picador, 2009),

[16] Maggie Hamilton, *What's Happening to Our Girls? Too Much, Too Soon - How our Kids are Overstimulated, Oversold and Oversexed.* (London: Penguin Group, 2009).

[17] I am indebted to many remarkable thinkers whose works I reference and relish throughout. Across the growing body of this work - from progressive feminist analyses to conservative and religious treatments - are some striking consensus that I will highlight throughout. Clearly, the issues at stake here are neither religious or nonreligious, conservative or liberal; these are human issues that anyone might appreciate. I have relied on a wide variety of sources, including personal interviews, group discussion, national surveys, self-help literature and philosophical accounts. Both secular and religious authors have been included in the conversation as well - always with an aim for the content included to be accessible to anyone.

[18] Barbara Dafoe Whitehead, *Why There Are No Good Men Left: The Romantic Plight of the New Single Woman* (New York: Broadway Books, 2003), 8.

[19] Wendy Walsh, *The 30-day Love Detox* (New York: Rodale, 2013), 24.

[20] Barbara Dafoe Whitehead, *Why There Are No Good Men Left: The Romantic Plight of the New Single Woman* (New York: Broadway Books, 2003), 11, 19, 97.

[21] Emphasis mine. Stephanie Coontz, *Marriage, a History: From Obedience to Intimacy, or How Love Conquered Marriage* (New York: Viking Books, 2005), 2, 4.

[21] Muriel Rukeyser, The Speed of Darkness (New York: Vintage, 1971).

[21] I identify with philosophical hermeneutics - where interpretations are understood to be directly relevant to the practicalities of citizens' actual experience and "lived out" moment by moment in tangible ways (see writings of Charles Taylor and Hans Gadamer).

Chapter 1

[1] Robert A. Johnson, *We: Understanding the Psychology of Romantic Love* (New York: HarperOne, 1985), xiii, 72.

[2] Sheff (2011)

[3] These lines from Cosette and Marius' romance in the musical Les Miserables

[4] Robert A. Johnson, *We: Understanding the Psychology of Romantic Love* (New York: HarperOne, 1985), 66, 163.

[5] Lori Gottlieb, *Marry Him: The Case for Settling for Mr. Good Enough* (New York: New American Library, 2010), 6.

[6] Robert A. Johnson, *We: Understanding the Psychology of Romantic Love* (New York: HarperOne, 1985), xiii, 96, 99.

[7] Simon May, *Love: A History* (London: Yale University Press, 2011), 180.

[8] Barbara Dafoe Whitehead, *Why There Are No Good Men Left: The Romantic Plight of the New Single Woman* (New York: Broadway Books, 2003), 105-106.

[9] Simon May, *Love: A History* (London: Yale University Press, 2011), 237.

[10] Ana Barrón López de Roda, et al. "Romantic beliefs and myths in Spain." *The Spanish Journal of Psychology*, 2(1), 64-73 (1999).

[11] This kind of intense and more demanding connection becomes more important than anything else. In this same survey, for instance, over 80% of women agreed it is more important to have a husband who can communicate about his deepest feelings than one who makes a good living. Barbara Dafoe Whitehead and David Popenoe, "Who Wants To Marry A Soul Mate? New Survey Findings on Young Adults' Attitudes about Love and Marriage" *The State of Our Unions* (Rutgers University, The National Marriage Project, 2001).

[12] Simon May, *Love: A History* (London: Yale University Press, 2011), 12.

[13] New Orleans lawyer Albert Janin - as cited in Stephanie Coontz, *Marriage, a History: From Obedience to Intimacy, or How Love Conquered Marriage* (New York: Viking Books, 2005). 147, 178.

[14] Stephanie Coontz, *Marriage, a History: From Obedience to Intimacy, or How Love Conquered Marriage* (New York: Viking Books, 2005), 15, 23.

[15] Simon May, *Love: A History* (London: Yale University Press, 2011), 13.

[16] Stephanie Coontz, *Marriage, a History: From Obedience to Intimacy, or How Love Conquered Marriage* (New York: Viking Books, 2005), 179.

[17] Robert A. Johnson, *We: Understanding the Psychology of Romantic Love* (New York: HarperOne, 1985), 43, 55, 58, 60, 96, 99.

[17] Robert A. Johnson, *We: Understanding the Psychology of Romantic Love* (New York: HarperOne, 1985), xiii, xiv.

Chapter 2

[1] This statement, often misattributed to Shakespeare, is actually a paraphrase of the "second noble truth" taught by Gautama Buddha - namely, that the main cause of suffering is "craving"- including both craving to have something and desire to avoid (aversion).

[2] Emphasis my own. Simon May, *Love: A History* (London: Yale University Press, 2011), 4, 239, 246.

[3] Simon May, *Love: A History* (London: Yale University Press, 2011), 4, 239, 246.

[4] Arland Thorton and Linda Young-DemMarco, "Four Decades of Trends in Attitudes Toward Family Issues in the United States," Journal of Marriage and Family 63 (2001).

[5] Robert A. Johnson, We: Understanding the Psychology of Romantic Love (New York: HarperOne, 1985), *61, 66-67, 94, 163.

[6] Robert Moore, A perpetually relevant, crucial study of how marriages have been formed throughout history, April 24, 2006, Amazon review of Stephanie Coontz, Marriage, a History: From Obedience to Intimacy, or How Love Conquered Marriage (New York: Viking Books, 2005) http://www.amazon.com/Marriage-History-How-Love-Conquered/product-reviews/014303667X

[7] Elizabeth Gilbert "Eat, Pray author: Why marriage?" Cnn.com (2010, Jan 25).

[8] Zygmunt Bauman, Liquid Love: On the Frailty of Human Bonds (Cambridge: Polity Press, 2003), 32.

[9] Wendy Walsh, The 30-day Love Detox (New York: Rodale, 2013), 110.

[10] Lori Gottlieb, Marry Him: The Case for Settling for Mr. Good Enough (New York: New American Library, 2010), 17-18.

[11] Read page 20-22 in her book - for a remarkable list of deal breakers! Lori Gottlieb, Marry Him: The Case for Settling for Mr. Good Enough (New York: New American Library, 2010).

[12] Lori Gottlieb, Marry Him: The Case for Settling for Mr. Good Enough (New York: New American Library, 2010), 29.

[13] Nancy Etcoff, Susie Orbach, Jennifer Scott and Heidi D'Agostino, "The Real Truth About Beauty: A Global Report Findings of the Global Study on Women, Beauty and Well-Being" StrategyOne, Dove Campaign for Real Beauty (2004), 13, 47.

[14] Nancy Etcoff, Susie Orbach, Jennifer Scott and Heidi D'Agostino, "The Real Truth About Beauty: A Global Report Findings of the Global Study on Women, Beauty and Well-Being" StrategyOne, Dove Campaign for Real Beauty (2004), 4.

[15] David M. Buss, et al., "A Half Century of Mate Preferences: The Cultural Evolution of Values," Journal of Marriage and the Family 63 (2001).

[16] Grace Gold, UCLA Student Kjerstin Gruys Swears Off Mirrors For A Year. Huffington Post (2011, August 8).

[17] Joan Jacobs Brumberg, The Body Project: An Intimate History of American Girls (New York: Vintage Books, 1998), 78.

[18] Joan Jacobs Brumberg, The Body Project: An Intimate History of American Girls (New York: Vintage Books, 1998), 23.

[19] Dawn Eden, The Thrill of the Chaste: Finding Fulfillment While Keeping Your Clothes On (Nashville, TN: Thomas Nelson, 2006), 37-38.

[20] Joan Jacobs Brumberg, The Body Project: An Intimate History of American Girls (New York: Vintage Books, 1998).

[21] Kirkus Review (1997) for Joan Jacobs Brumberg, *The Body Project: An Intimate History of American Girls* (New York: Vintage Books, 1998).

[22] Leslie Ludy, *The Lost Art of True Beauty* (Grace Harvest House Publishers, 2010).

[23] What about expectations for men? While they also clearly exist, there is really no comparison to those being asked of women. To underscore the point, one author mused about what the world would be like if men had to conform to similar kinds of standards for appearance:

(1) To keep up with the beauty ideal...men have to wax or shave their forearms weekly. No hairy arms or knuckles. To avoid it, some men just keep their sleeves rolled down - even in the summer. But if they want to wear short sleeves, or get a date with a woman, they absolutely have to be smooth and shaven from the elbow down. Sure, they could rebel, and show up to work hairy, but... it'd be a *statement*.

(2) There simply aren't gray-haired men. Women can let themselves go gray, or even have white hair - people think they look smarter, hotter, more "distinguished." But men? Never. So guys of a certain age who don't want to look like they've passed their "use-by" date are always running off at lunchtime to get their roots done.

(3) Being bald or even having thinning hair is just...unacceptable....Sure, some guys go natural, but they tend to be Men's Studies professors at liberal universities....The salons are just full of men trying to get that fashionable, thick, wavy hair women like so much. Some say they're doing it for themselves.

(4) Any guy shorter than 5 feet 10 feels uncomfortable...So, most short men wear big wedge heels....Once again, a guy could choose not to conform, but it might be tough when all the other men are wearing heels. Plus, lots of guys like the way they look with longer legs.

(5) Sitcoms would feature couples where the men are tall, muscular, and hot, while the wives are chubby and witty...Because the style for men...is to wear skin-tight T shirts, men are obsessed with having a flat stomach. Men... Salons, cosmetic-surgery offices and Weight Watchers meetings would be filled with men who spend a fortune trying to get that iconic masculine "V" shape women crave. They'd exhaust themselves trying to juggle family and work. Some would slowly give up. Some men...would rebel. They'd ask: why won't women love us for who we are, or for our money, or our success, instead of our flowing hair and broad shoulders? Women shrug would their shoulders. "We can't help it," they say. "It's pure biology and evolution." From: Schrobsdorff, S. "What if men everywhere had to conform to beauty standards set by women?" *Man Up Newsweek Special Addition: The beauty advantage.* (2010, Jul 19).

[24] Natasha Walter (2010) Living Dolls.Virago Hardbacks.

[25] Dawn Eden, *The Thrill of the Chaste: Finding Fulfillment While Keeping Your Clothes On* (Nashville, TN: Thomas Nelson, 2006), 148.

[26] Dawn Eden, *The Thrill of the Chaste: Finding Fulfillment While Keeping Your Clothes On* (Nashville, TN: Thomas Nelson, 2006), xi.

[27] Shaun Dreisbach, "5 secrets of body-confident women: Glamour survey of 16,000 women shows how to break the body-hating cycle," Glamour Magazine, (March 27, 2009).

[28] Jessica Weiner, author of "Life Doesn't Begin 5 Pounds From Now" as cited in Shaun Dreisbach, "5 secrets of body-confident women: Glamour survey of 16,000 women shows how to break the body-hating cycle," Glamour Magazine, (March 27, 2009).

[29] Nancy Etcoff, Susie Orbach, Jennifer Scott and Heidi D'Agostino, "The Real Truth About Beauty: A Global Report Findings of the Global Study on Women, Beauty and Well-Being" StrategyOne, Dove Campaign for Real Beauty (2004), 4.

[30] Press Release, "Negative Feelings About Their Looks Cause Majority of Girls to Disengage From Life" Dove (2004).
Campaign for Real Beauty Global Study Reveals

[31] Nancy Etcoff, Susie Orbach, Jennifer Scott and Heidi D'Agostino, "The Real Truth About Beauty: A Global Report Findings of the Global Study on Women, Beauty and Well-Being" StrategyOne, Dove Campaign for Real Beauty (2004), 5, 25.

[32] Simon May, *Love: A History* (London: Yale University Press, 2011), 237.

[33] Robert A. Johnson, *We: Understanding the Psychology of Romantic Love* (New York: HarperOne, 1985), 182.

[34] Stephanie Coontz, *Marriage, a History: From Obedience to Intimacy, or How Love Conquered Marriage* (New York: Viking Books, 2005), 250.

[35] Cited in Albert Y. Hsu, *Singles at the Crossroads* (Downer's Grove, IL: InterVarsity Press, 1997), 70.

[36] Wendy Walsh, *The 30-day Love Detox* (New York: Rodale, 2013), 43 - commenting on the work of David Buss and Martie G. Haselton.

[37] Sonja Lyubomirsky, *The Myths of Happiness. What Should Make You Happy, but Doesn't, What Shouldn't Make You Happy, but Does* (London: Penguin Press, 2013).

[38] Wendy Walsh, *The 30-day Love Detox* (New York: Rodale, 2013), **

[39] Stephanie Coontz, *Marriage, a History: From Obedience to Intimacy, or How Love Conquered Marriage* (New York: Viking Books, 2005), 204.

[40] Stephanie Coontz, *Marriage, a History: From Obedience to Intimacy, or How Love Conquered Marriage* (New York: Viking Books, 2005), 23.

Chapter 3

[1] Robert A. Johnson, *We: Understanding the Psychology of Romantic Love* (New York: HarperOne, 1985), 61.

[2] Robert A. Johnson, *We: Understanding the Psychology of Romantic Love* (New York: HarperOne, 1985), 57.

[3] M. Scott Peck, *The Road Less Travelled* (Touchstone, 1988), 89.

[4] Erich Fromm, *The Art of Loving* (New York: Harper Perennial, 1956/2006), 92.

[5] M. Scott Peck, *The Road Less Travelled* (Touchstone, 1988), 3.

[6] Zygmunt Bauman, *Liquid Love: On the Frailty of Human Bonds* (Cambridge: Polity Press, 2003), 12.

[7] Erich Fromm, *The Art of Loving* (New York: Harper Perennial, 1956/2006), 2, 52.

[8] Erich Fromm, *The Art of Loving* (New York: Harper Perennial, 1956/2006), *1, 52.

[9] Albert Y. Hsu, *Singles at the Crossroads* (Downer's Grove, IL: InterVarsity Press, 1997), 139-140.

[10] Patricia Noller, "What is this thing called love? Defining the love that supports marriage and family," Personal Relationships , 3(1), 1996, 107.

[11] Erich Fromm, *The Art of Loving* (New York: Harper Perennial, 1956/2006), 84.

[12] Albert Y. Hsu, *Singles at the Crossroads* (Downer's Grove, IL: InterVarsity Press, 1997), 140.

[13] Dawn Eden, *The Thrill of the Chaste: Finding Fulfillment While Keeping Your Clothes On* (Nashville, TN: Thomas Nelson, 2006), 116.

[14] Erich Fromm, *The Art of Loving* (New York: Harper Perennial, 1956/2006), 4.

[15] Zygmunt Bauman, *Liquid Love: On the Frailty of Human Bonds* (Cambridge: Polity Press, 2003), 12.

[16] A paraphrase of M. Scott Peck, *The Road Less Travelled* (Touchstone, 1988), 89.

[17] Zygmunt Bauman, *Liquid Love: On the Frailty of Human Bonds* (Cambridge: Polity Press, 2003), 7.

[18] S.J. Jones , *Antonio Gramsci* (Routledge, 2006), 9.

[19] Robert A. Johnson, *We: Understanding the Psychology of Romantic Love* (New York: HarperOne, 1985), 103.

[20] Robert A. Johnson, *We: Understanding the Psychology of Romantic Love* (New York: HarperOne, 1985), 110.

[21] Ana Barrón López de Roda, et al. "Romantic beliefs and myths in Spain." The Spanish Journal of Psychology, 2(1), 64-73 (1999).

[22] F. F. Furstenberg (1990). Divorce and the American family. Annual Review of Sociology, 16, 379-403.

[23] Simon May, *Love: A History* (London: Yale University Press, 2011), 175, 178.

[24] Robert A. Johnson, *We: Understanding the Psychology of Romantic Love* (New York: HarperOne, 1985), 57.

[25] Albert Y. Hsu, *Singles at the Crossroads* (Downer's Grove, IL: InterVarsity Press, 1997), 139.

[26] Patricia Noller, "What is this thing called love? Defining the love that supports marriage and family," Personal Relationships , 3(1), 1996, 108.

[27] Robert A. Johnson, We: Understanding the Psychology of Romantic Love (New York: HarperOne, 1985), 134, 138-139.

[28] Simon May, Love: A History (London: Yale University Press, 2011), 179.

[29] Menno AartsenSeattle, WA commenting on * Alex Williams "The End of Courtship?" New York Times (Jan 11, 2013).

[30] Wendy Walsh, The 30-day Love Detox (New York: Rodale, 2013), 8.

[31] M. Scott Peck, The Road Less Travelled (Touchstone, 1988), 89.

[32] M. Scott Peck, The Road Less Travelled (Touchstone, 1988), 89.

Chapter 4

[1] Barbara Dafoe Whitehead, Why There Are No Good Men Left: The Romantic Plight of the New Single Woman (New York: Broadway Books, 2003), 38.

[2] Peggy Fletcher Stack, "Why Young LDS Men are Pushing Back Marriage" The Salt Lake Tribune (2011, April 19).

[3] Leigh Dethman and Nicole Warburton, "LDS and Single." Deseret Morning News. (2007, Mar 31).

[4] Stephanie Coontz, Marriage, a History: From Obedience to Intimacy, or How Love Conquered Marriage (New York: Viking Books, 2005), 100, 180, 185, 201. The citation about a "tremendous personal flaw" on page 100 originally comes from (G, The Bourgeois Experience).

[5] Robert A. Johnson, We: Understanding the Psychology of Romantic Love (New York: HarperOne, 1985), 78.

[6] (Dollahite, 2002).

[7] (AnnaliseUSA). *

[8] Albert Y. Hsu, Singles at the Crossroads (Downer's Grove, IL: InterVarsity Press, 1997), 147.

[9] Lori Gottlieb, Marry Him: The Case for Settling for Mr. Good Enough (New York: New American Library, 2010), 19, 23.

[10] Barbara Dafoe Whitehead, Why There Are No Good Men Left: The Romantic Plight of the New Single Woman (New York: Broadway Books, 2003), 51.

[11] Amato, Paul & Allan Booth (1997) A Generation at Risk: Growing up in an era of family upheaval. Harvard University Press, Cambridge MA.

[12] Barbara Dafoe Whitehead and David Popenoe, "Who Wants To Marry A Soul Mate? New Survey Findings on Young Adults' Attitudes about Love and Marriage" The State of Our Unions (Rutgers University, The National Marriage Project, 2001), 18.

[13] As cited in Barbara Dafoe Whitehead and David Popenoe, "Who Wants To Marry A Soul Mate? New Survey Findings on Young Adults' Attitudes about Love and Marriage" *The State of Our Unions* (Rutgers University, The *National Marriage* Project, 2001), 16.

[14] Andrew Hacker, *Mismatch: The Growing Gulf Between Women and Men* (Scribner, 2007).

[15] Barbara Dafoe Whitehead, *Why There Are No Good Men Left: The Romantic Plight of the New Single Woman* (New York: Broadway Books, 2003), 175.

[16] Barry Schwartz, *The Paradox of Choice: Why More Is Less* (New York: Harper Perennial, 2005).

[17] Stephanie Coontz, *Marriage, a History: From Obedience to Intimacy, or How Love Conquered Marriage* (New York: Viking Books, 2005), 179.

[18] Zygmunt Bauman, *Liquid Love: On the Frailty of Human Bonds* (Cambridge: Polity Press, 2003), xi, 47, 58, 90.

[19] Cited in Zygmunt Bauman, *Liquid Love: On the Frailty of Human Bonds* (Cambridge: Polity Press, 2003), x, 11, 12*

[20] Zygmunt Bauman, *Liquid Love: On the Frailty of Human Bonds* (Cambridge: Polity Press, 2003), *

[21] Robert A. Johnson, *We: Understanding the Psychology of Romantic Love* (New York: HarperOne, 1985), 140.

[22] Zygmunt Bauman, *Liquid Love: On the Frailty of Human Bonds* (Cambridge: Polity Press, 2003), 12-13, 15, 90.

[23] Barbara Dafoe Whitehead, *Why There Are No Good Men Left: The Romantic Plight of the New Single Woman* (New York: Broadway Books, 2003), 130.

[24] Joshua Sky as cited in Alex Williams "The End of Courtship?" *New York Times* (Jan 11, 2013).

[25] Shani Silver as cited in Alex Williams "The End of Courtship?" *New York Times* (Jan 11, 2013).

[26] Anna Goldfarb as cited in Alex Williams "The End of Courtship?" *New York Times* (Jan 11, 2013).

[27] Alex Williams "The End of Courtship?" *New York Times* (Jan 11, 2013).

[28] Wendy Walsh, *The 30-day Love Detox* (New York: Rodale, 2013), 4.

[29] Lex Edness as cited in Alex Williams "The End of Courtship?" *New York Times* (Jan 11, 2013).

[30] DavidLos Angeles, CA* commenting on Alex Williams "The End of Courtship?" *New York Times* (Jan 11, 2013).

[31] Barbara Dafoe Whitehead, *Why There Are No Good Men Left: The Romantic Plight of the New Single Woman* (New York: Broadway Books, 2003), 13, 115.

[32] Alex Williams "The End of Courtship?" *New York Times* (Jan 11, 2013).

[33] Holman&Sillars 2011 Health Communication, 27(2), 205-216.

[34] Wendy Walsh, *The 30-day Love Detox* (New York: Rodale, 2013), 77, 123.

[35] Whitehead's elaboration of this process is interesting:

A boyfriend's obligations have been clearly defined by this ladder of commitment: his role is to take romantic initiative at every step in the dating relationship. He has to strike up a conversation, make a phone call, pay for a date, and win the affections of his girlfriend first, and then, gain the approval of her family and friends. The crucial male romantic initiative is the marriage proposal. Once a man is secure in his girlfriend's affections and reasonably confident of her likely consideration, or consent, to marriage, his responsibility is to propose marriage and present her with a tangible symbol of his commitment, usually an engagement ring. This tradition has many variations, of course, and the proposal often evolves slowly as a mutual understanding rather than erupting as a "pop the question" surprise. However, the romantic responsibility exists, not even so much for the sake of propriety or tradition, as much as for the sake of a young woman's feelings of being chosen and special above all others. In this ladder, each rung also has been surrounded by symbols and rituals of commitment, especially as couples progress toward marriage. Rings and engagements are important, because they enable couples who are past the stage of infatuation to have a shared and unambiguous understanding of their relationship. Moreover, they are public, so they announce this intention to the larger social world. They bring third parties - notably family, close friends, and social acquaintances - into the relationship as sources of advice, support, and feedback. This is especially important in a mating system where the choice of a mate is made freely, mutually, and independently by the couple themselves. Third parties can support, advise, and sometimes offer cautions before the couple reaches the altar. Moreover, such courtship practices are designed to translate the subjective state of being in love into objective expressions of commitment. In this way, they reduce the chances for confusion, misrepresentation, or ambiguity about the nature and future purpose of the romance.... Romantic relationships are notoriously susceptible to deliberate deception, accidental miscommunication, and wishful thinking....These rituals provide objective and commonly recognized measures of "where the relationship is headed," so everyone is on the same page. Barbara Dafoe Whitehead, *Why There Are No Good Men Left: The Romantic Plight of the New Single Woman* (New York: Broadway Books, 2003), 108-109.

[36] Barbara Dafoe Whitehead, *Why There Are No Good Men Left: The Romantic Plight of the New Single Woman* (New York: Broadway Books, 2003), 100, 105.

[37] Kay Hymowitz, Jason S. Carroll, W. Bradford Wilcox and Kelleen Kaye, "Knot Yet: The Benefits and Costs of Delayed Marriage in America," *National Marriage Project at the University of Virginia* (2013), citation on this webpage.

[38] Barbara Dafoe Whitehead, *Why There Are No Good Men Left: The Romantic Plight of the New Single Woman* (New York: Broadway Books, 2003), 123.

[39] Barbara Dafoe Whitehead, *Why There Are No Good Men Left: The Romantic Plight of the New Single Woman* (New York: Broadway Books, 2003), 129.

[40] Barbara Dafoe Whitehead, *Why There Are No Good Men Left: The Romantic Plight of the New Single Woman* (New York: Broadway Books, 2003), 141-142

[41] Wendy Walsh, *The 30-day Love Detox* (New York: Rodale, 2013), xiv, 14, 50.

[42] Barbara Dafoe Whitehead, *Why There Are No Good Men Left: The Romantic Plight of the New Single Woman* (New York: Broadway Books, 2003), 123.

[43] Wendy Walsh, *The 30-day Love Detox* (New York: Rodale, 2013), xiv, 14, 50.

[44] Meg Jay p. 190 *Defining Decade*

[45] Zygmunt Bauman, *Liquid Love: On the Frailty of Human Bonds* (Cambridge: Polity Press, 2003), 12.

[46] Robert A. Johnson, *We: Understanding the Psychology of Romantic Love* (New York: HarperOne, 1985), viii, xiv.

[47] Zygmunt Bauman, *Liquid Love: On the Frailty of Human Bonds* (Cambridge: Polity Press, 2003), 21-22.

[48] Robert A. Johnson, *We: Understanding the Psychology of Romantic Love* (New York: HarperOne, 1985), 44-45, 102.

[49] Barbara Dafoe Whitehead, *Why There Are No Good Men Left: The Romantic Plight of the New Single Woman* (New York: Broadway Books, 2003), 46-47.

Chapter 5

[1] Barbara Dafoe Whitehead, *Why There Are No Good Men Left: The Romantic Plight of the New Single Woman* (New York: Broadway Books, 2003), 167.

[2] Barbara Dafoe Whitehead, *Why There Are No Good Men Left: The Romantic Plight of the New Single Woman* (New York: Broadway Books, 2003), 30, 31, 45, 112-113

[3] Barbara Dafoe Whitehead, *Why There Are No Good Men Left: The Romantic Plight of the New Single Woman* (New York: Broadway Books, 2003), 51.

[4] Ellen Fein and Sherrie Schneider, *The Rules: Time-Tested Secrets for Capturing the Heart of Mr. Right* (New York: Warner Books, 1995; New York, Warner Books Paperback, 1996), 3.

[5] Donna Freitas, *The End of Sex: How Hookup Culture is Leaving a Generation Unhappy, Sexually Unfulfilled, and Confused About Intimacy* (Basic Books, 2013).

[6] Zygmunt Bauman, *Liquid Love: On the Frailty of Human Bonds* (Cambridge: Polity Press, 2003), 5.

[7] Summary statement from Colleen Mondor's Booklist Review of Susie Orbach, *Bodies* (Bodies. New York: Picador, 2009).

[8] American Psychological Association, Task Force on the Sexualization of Girls. (2010). Report of the APA Task Force on the Sexualization of Girls.

[9] Schooler, D., & Ward, L. M. (2006). Average Joes: Men's relationships with media, real bodies, and sexuality. *Psychology of Men & Masculinity*, 7(1), 27–41.

[10] Hamilton, M. (2009). *What's Happening to Our Girls? Too Much, Too Soon - how our kids are overstimulated, oversold and oversexed.* Penguin Group.

[11] Kerner, K. (2011, Jan 20). How porn is changing our sex lives. CNN http://thechart.blogs.cnn.com/2011/01/20/how-porn-is-changing-our-sex-lives/

[12] Naomi Wolf (October 20, 2003). "The Porn Myth". New York Magazine. Archived from the original on September 24, 2012.

[13] Ana Barrón López de Roda, et al. "Romantic beliefs and myths in Spain." The Spanish Journal of Psychology, 2(1), 1999, 71.

[14] Matthew Stumphy, "The Biggest Mistake Made by Single Mormons Results"(2009, Aug 13/Sep 6/Oct 20) www.gurustump.com

[15] Robert A. Johnson, *We: Understanding the Psychology of Romantic Love* (New York: HarperOne, 1985), 100-101, 129.

[16] Robert A. Johnson, *We: Understanding the Psychology of Romantic Love* (New York: HarperOne, 1985), 140.

[17] Gail Saltz TODAYupdated 5/15/2007 5:20:19 PM ET Do men cheat for the thrill? Or the sex? today.com

[18] Italics mine. Robert A. Johnson, *We: Understanding the Psychology of Romantic Love* (New York: HarperOne, 1985), 129, 140, 144-145.

[19] Erich Fromm, *The Art of Loving* (New York: Harper Perennial, 1956/2006), 93.

[20] Naomi Wolf, *The Beauty Myth: How Images of Beauty are Used Against Women* (New York: Harper Perennial, 1992/2002), 174, 177.

[21] Naomi Wolf, The Beauty Myth: How Images of Beauty are Used Against Women (New York: Harper Perennial, 1992/2002), 174.

[22] Erich Fromm, *The Art of Loving* (New York: Harper Perennial, 1956/2006), 25.

[23] Robert A. Johnson, *We: Understanding the Psychology of Romantic Love* (New York: HarperOne, 1985), 140.

Chapter 6

[1] Simon May, *Love: A History* (London: Yale University Press, 2011), 7, 241.

[2] Robert A. Johnson, *We: Understanding the Psychology of Romantic Love* (New York: HarperOne, 1985), 110.

[3] Courtney, C. (2002). Table for One: The Savvy Girl's Guide to Singleness Baker 112, 117.

[4] John A. Sanford, *The Invisible Partners: How the Male and Female in Each of Us Affects Our Relationships*, (Paulist Press, 1980), 19.

[5] Barbara Dafoe Whitehead and David Popenoe, "Who Wants To Marry A Soul Mate? New Survey Findings on Young Adults' Attitudes about Love and Marriage" *The State of Our Unions* (Rutgers University, The *National Marriage* Project, 2001).

[6] Attributed to Henri Frederic Amiel

[7] Nancy Etcoff, Susie Orbach, Jennifer Scott and Heidi D'Agostino, "The Real Truth About Beauty: A Global Report Findings of the Global Study on Women, Beauty and Well-Being" StrategyOne, Dove Campaign for Real Beauty (2004), 1, 5, 35-36.

[8] While physical appearance and being in good shape were also identified as enhancing feelings of beauty, interestingly enough, these body-specific factors mattered less than social and emotional factors. See: Nancy Etcoff, Susie Orbach, Jennifer Scott and Heidi D'Agostino, "The Real Truth About Beauty: A Global Report Findings of the Global Study on Women, Beauty and Well-Being" StrategyOne, Dove Campaign for Real Beauty (2004), 29-30.

[9] Nancy Etcoff, Susie Orbach, Jennifer Scott and Heidi D'Agostino, "The Real Truth About Beauty: A Global Report Findings of the Global Study on Women, Beauty and Well-Being" StrategyOne, Dove Campaign for Real Beauty (2004), 5.

[10] Caitlin Boyle, *Operation Beautiful: Transforming the Way You See Yourself One Post-it Note at a Time.* (Gotham, 2010).

[11] Spencer W. Kimball, *Faith Precedes the Miracle,* (Salt Lake City: Deseret Book, 1972), 157-159.

[12] Ballard, 2002*

[13] Geneen Roth, *Women Food and God: An Unexpected Path to Almost Everything,* (Simon & Schuster, 2011), 174-175.

[14] Nancy Etcoff, Susie Orbach, Jennifer Scott and Heidi D'Agostino, "The Real Truth About Beauty: A Global Report Findings of the Global Study on Women, Beauty and Well-Being" StrategyOne, Dove Campaign for Real Beauty (2004), 1, 5, 35-36.

[15] Fisher 2004* and Brehm et al. (2002). Gaunt, R. (2006). Couple Similarity and Marital Satisfaction: Are Similar Spouses Happier? Journal of Personality, 74(5), 1401-1420.

[16] Simon May, *Love: A History* (London: Yale University Press, 2011), 8.

Chapter 7

[1] Simon May, *Love: A History* (London: Yale University Press, 2011), 13.

[2] Lori Gottlieb, *Marry Him: The Case for Settling for Mr. Good Enough* (New York: New American Library, 2010), 10.

[3] Italics mine. Lori Gottlieb, *Marry Him: The Case for Settling for Mr. Good Enough* (New York: New American Library, 2010), 22.

[4] Saraceno, The Italian Family, in Antoine Prost & Gerard Vincent, eds., A History of Private Life: Riddles of Identity in Modern Times (Cambridge, Mass.: Belknap Press, 1991), (Coontz, 2005, p. 487.

[5] Robert A. Johnson, *We: Understanding the Psychology of Romantic Love* (New York: HarperOne, 1985), xii.

[6] Robert A. Johnson, *We: Understanding the Psychology of Romantic Love* (New York: HarperOne, 1985), xi.

[7] Cited in Shostak, 1981, p. 268

[8] Captain Corelli's Mandolin.

[9] Stephanie Coontz, *Marriage, a History: From Obedience to Intimacy, or How Love Conquered Marriage* (New York: Viking Books, 2005), 184.

[10] George Jean Nathan

[11] Peter J. Marston, et al., "The subjective experience of intimacy, passion, and commitment in heterosexual loving relationships. "Personal Relationships 5(1), 1998, 15-30.

[12] Judith A. Feeney & Patricia Noller - Attachment style as a predictor of adult romantic relationships. Journal of personality and Social Psychology, 1990 Vol 58(2), Feb 1990, 281-291.

[13] Judith A. Feeney & Patricia Noller. Attachment style and verbal descriptions of romantic partners. Journal of Social and Personal Relationships May 1991 vol. 8 no. 2 187-215

[14] Robert J. Sternberg, Karin Weis Eds. *The New Psychology of Love* (New Haven: Yale University Press, 2008), 101.

[15] And, of course - what counts as 'passion' is also worth talking about. One author cautions, "We must not assume that someone whose feelings are modulated and controlled is not a passionate person." Indeed, he notes, "The fact that a feeling is uncontrolled is no indication whatsoever that it is any deeper than a feeling that is disciplined." M. Scott Peck, *The Road Less Travelled* (Touchstone, 1988), 156.

[16] Robert A. Johnson, *We: Understanding the Psychology of Romantic Love* (New York: HarperOne, 1985), 132.
More than simply quantitative lessening of expectation in the 'amount of feeling,' this involves a qualitative shift in the feeling-to-be-desired - from a single-minded attention to sexual intensity of feeling, to an appreciation of the broader spectrum of feelings that goes beyond the physical to the whole person.

[17] Nancy Etcoff, Susie Orbach, Jennifer Scott and Heidi D'Agostino, "The Real Truth About Beauty: A Global Report Findings of the Global Study on Women, Beauty and Well-Being" StrategyOne, Dove Campaign for Real Beauty (2004), 5-6.

[18] First phrase from Publisher Weekly's Review of Ophira Edut, Ed. *Body Outlaws: Rewriting the Rules of Beauty and Body Image. [Formerly Adios Barbie]* (Jackson, TN:

Seal Press, 2004), http://www.publishersweekly.com/978-1-58005-016-6 Second phrase from the website page, "About the book" http://www.bodyoutlaws.com/about.html

[19] Nancy Etcoff, Susie Orbach, Jennifer Scott and Heidi D'Agostino, "The Real Truth About Beauty: A Global Report Findings of the Global Study on Women, Beauty and Well-Being" StrategyOne, Dove Campaign for Real Beauty (2004), 3-4.

[20] Hinckley, G. B. (1992, Mar). This I Believe

[21] Ophira Edut, Ed. *Body Outlaws: Rewriting the Rules of Beauty and Body Image.* (Jackson, TN: Seal Press, 2004), text from website page, "About the book" http://www.bodyoutlaws.com/about.html

[22] Nancy Etcoff, Susie Orbach, Jennifer Scott and Heidi D'Agostino, "The Real Truth About Beauty: A Global Report Findings of the Global Study on Women, Beauty and Well-Being" StrategyOne, Dove Campaign for Real Beauty (2004), 6.

[23] Nancy Etcoff, Susie Orbach, Jennifer Scott and Heidi D'Agostino, "The Real Truth About Beauty: A Global Report Findings of the Global Study on Women, Beauty and Well-Being" StrategyOne, Dove Campaign for Real Beauty (2004), 42.

[24] Lori Gottlieb, Marry Him: The Case for Settling for Mr. Good Enough (New York: New American Library, 2010), 27.

[25] Lori Gottlieb, Marry Him: The Case for Settling for Mr. Good Enough (New York: New American Library, 2010), 21.

[26] Lori Gottlieb, *Marry Him: The Case for Settling for Mr. Good Enough* (New York: New American Library, 2010), 23.

[27] (animaguskatt, 2011).

[28] Lori Gottlieb, Marry Him: The Case for Settling for Mr. Good Enough (New York: New American Library, 2010), 12

[29] Lori Gottlieb, *Marry Him: The Case for Settling for Mr. Good Enough* (New York: New American Library, 2010), 20.

[30] As cited in Wendy Walsh, *The 30-day Love Detox* (New York: Rodale, 2013), 110.

[31] Lori Gottlieb, *Marry Him: The Case for Settling for Mr. Good Enough* (New York: New American Library, 2010), 31.

[32] Lori Gottlieb, *Marry Him: The Case for Settling for Mr. Good Enough* (New York: New American Library, 2010), 11.

[33] Lori Gottlieb, *Marry Him: The Case for Settling for Mr. Good Enough* (New York: New American Library, 2010), 9.

[34] Lori Gottlieb, *Marry Him: The Case for Settling for Mr. Good Enough* (New York: New American Library, 2010), 25

[35] Stephanie Coontz, *Marriage, a History: From Obedience to Intimacy, or How Love Conquered Marriage* (New York: Viking Books, 2005), 183.

[36] Lori Gottlieb, *Marry Him: The Case for Settling for Mr. Good Enough* (New York: New American Library, 2010), 11.

[37] Lori Gottlieb, *Marry Him: The Case for Settling for Mr. Good Enough* (New York: New American Library, 2010), 24.

[38] Alex Williams "The End of Courtship?" *New York Times* (Jan 11, 2013).

[39] Wendy Walsh, *The 30-day Love Detox* (New York: Rodale, 2013), 204, 211

[40] Betsy Hart (March 22, 2013) Dating no longer a path to marriage, and women partly to blame Scripps Howard News Service

[41] JulesHalifax, NSNYT Pick Jan. 12, 2013 comment on Alex Williams "The End of Courtship?" *New York Times* (Jan 11, 2013).

[42] MassachusettsNYT Pick Jan. 12, 2013 comment on Alex Williams "The End of Courtship?" *New York Times* (Jan 11, 2013).

[43] Betsy Hart (March 22, 2013) Dating no longer a path to marriage, and women partly to blame Scripps Howard News Service

[44] Betsy Hart (March 22, 2013) Dating no longer a path to marriage, and women partly to blame Scripps Howard News Service

[45] LisaVermont*

[46] Mark Regnerus and Jeremy Uecker, *Premarital Sex in a America: How Young Americans Meet, Mate and Think about Marrying.* (New York: Oxford University Press, 2011).

[47] As cited in Wendy Walsh, *The 30-day Love Detox* (New York: Rodale, 2013), 138.

[48] Wendy Walsh, *The 30-day Love Detox* (New York: Rodale, 2013), 129.

[49] As cited in Wendy Walsh, *The 30-day Love Detox* (New York: Rodale, 2013), 149.

[50] Wendy Walsh, *The 30-day Love Detox* (New York: Rodale, 2013), 156.

[51] Cited in Wendy Walsh, *The 30-day Love Detox* (New York: Rodale, 2013), 130.

[52] Wendy Walsh, *The 30-day Love Detox* (New York: Rodale, 2013), 72.

[53] In a book targeted to a female audience - Walsh's language is gender specific: "He's gotta be right for you and your family plans. Or he's gotta go." She explains: "We need to clear away the clouds of alcohol, sex hormones, and tech addiction . We need to see [people] more clearly. And we need remedies for all our withdrawal symptoms. Then, we can reintroduce love to our diets - that is, [partners] with high emotional nutrition. This is how we'll take back control of our relationships." She admits to some real "aftershock of pulling yourself off the high-supply sexual market." She predicts the result: "Slowly, almost without your noticing, that bandwidth of male attention will begin to shrink. You'll log into Facebook and see fewer messages. Texts from players and commitment phobes who used to chirp out daily on your smartphone will disappear for days at a time. And then weeks. And then, they'll drop off completely. Ladies, this won't feel good. You might feel lonely and abandoned and find yourself 'just browsing' online dating sites. You might find yourself with an urge to go stir up some male attention, but I advise against this. Things will slow down. Your life will become quieter. You'll feel the full impact of the backward sexual economy. Most men will

move on to women who'll give them easy sex. But you don't need most men. You don't need them for your self-esteem. You don't need them for financial support. You don't need them for sexual pleasure...You don't need most men for your self-worth or even for your happiness. You just need one man for a healthy relationship. Take a deep breath." Wendy Walsh, The 30-day Love Detox (New York: Rodale, 2013), 50, 131, 137, 157.

[54] Wendy Walsh, The 30-day Love Detox (New York: Rodale, 2013), 127, 158, 163.

Chapter 8

[1] Erich Fromm, The Art of Loving (New York: Harper Perennial, 1956/2006), 21, 83, 120.

[2] Erich Fromm, The Art of Loving (New York: Harper Perennial, 1956/2006), 25.

[3] M. Scott Peck, The Road Less Travelled (Touchstone, 1988), 118-119.

[4] Stephen Kendrick and Alex Kendrick, The Love Dare (Nashville: B&H Books, 2008, viii.

[5] Erich Fromm, The Art of Loving (New York: Harper Perennial, 1956/2006), 5, 57.

[6] Simon May, Love: A History (London: Yale University Press, 2011), 243.

[7] Simon May, Love: A History (London: Yale University Press, 2011), 196-197.

[8] Robert A. Johnson, We: Understanding the Psychology of Romantic Love (New York: HarperOne, 1985), *

[9] Robert A. Johnson, We: Understanding the Psychology of Romantic Love (New York: HarperOne, 1985), 102-103.

[10] Gordon B. Hinckley. What God hath joined together. General Conference. 1991

[11] Erich Fromm, The Art of Loving (New York: Harper Perennial, 1956/2006), 21, 83, 120.

[12] M. Scott Peck, The Road Less Travelled (Touchstone, 1988), 119.

[13] M. Scott Peck, The Road Less Travelled (Touchstone, 1988), 116-117.

[14] Cited in Stephanie Coontz, Marriage, a History: From Obedience to Intimacy, or How Love Conquered Marriage (New York: Viking Books, 2005), 178.

[15] Barbara Fredrickson (2013, January 24). 10 things you might not know about love Special to CNN

[16] Fredrickson, B. (2013, January 24). 10 things you might not know about love Special to CNN

[17] Although framed for married couples, this book could be used by anyone dating as well. Similarly, while this book is written for a Christian audience, but has potential applicability far beyond that. (see http://thelovedarebook.com).

[18] Erich Fromm, The Art of Loving (New York: Harper Perennial, 1956/2006), 78.

Chapter 9

[1] M. Scott Peck, *The Road Less Travelled* (Touchstone, 1988), 88.

[2] M. Scott Peck, *The Road Less Travelled* (Touchstone, 1988), 88.

[3] Erich Fromm, *The Art of Loving* (New York: Harper Perennial, 1956/2006), 4. 49.

[4] Robert A. Johnson, *We: Understanding the Psychology of Romantic Love* (New York: HarperOne, 1985), 184-185.

[5] Don't get me wrong - this isn't about giving up on someone who is sincere about improving their life and making changes. But make sure he or she is the real deal. Dramatic promises of future improvement are not enough to give yourself to someone. And desperation to not be lonely is not a reason to sweep fears underneath the rug. As hard as it might be to be single, it is much, much harder to suddenly find yourself in a painful relationship.

[6] Referencing Winston Churchill's famous declaration: "The whole fury and might of the enemy must very soon be turned on us. Hitler knows that he will have to break us in this island or lose the war. If we can stand up to him, all Europe may be freed and the life of the world may move forward into broad, sunlit uplands. But if we fail, then the whole world, ...all that we have known and cared for, will sink into the abyss of a new dark age...Let us therefore brace ourselves to our duties, and so bear ourselves, that if the British Empire and its Commonwealth last for a thousand years, men will still say, This was their finest hour."

[7] Robert A. Johnson, *We: Understanding the Psychology of Romantic Love* (New York: HarperOne, 1985), 72, 100-101, 129.

[8] Robert A. Johnson, *We: Understanding the Psychology of Romantic Love* (New York: HarperOne, 1985), 44.

[9] Robert A. Johnson, *We: Understanding the Psychology of Romantic Love* (New York: HarperOne, 1985), 184-185.

[10] Robert A. Johnson, *We: Understanding the Psychology of Romantic Love* (New York: HarperOne, 1985), 67, 72, 100-101.

[11] Robert A. Johnson, *We: Understanding the Psychology of Romantic Love* (New York: HarperOne, 1985), 100-101, 129.

[12] M. Scott Peck, *The Road Less Travelled* (Touchstone, 1988), 91-92.

[13] Robert A. Johnson, *We: Understanding the Psychology of Romantic Love* (New York: HarperOne, 1985), 112, 140-141.

[14] Robert A. Johnson, *We: Understanding the Psychology of Romantic Love* (New York: HarperOne, 1985), 130, 148.

[15] Stephen Kendrick and Alex Kendrick, *The Love Dare* (Nashville: B&H Books, 2008), 211.

[16] Erich Fromm, *The Art of Loving* (New York: Harper Perennial, 1956/2006), 4, 49.

[17] Italics mine. M. Scott Peck, *The Road Less Travelled* (Touchstone, 1988), 84-85.

[18] Jane E. Brody, "That Loving Feeling Takes a Lot of Work," New York Times Blog, January 14, 2013.

[19] Sonja Lyubomirsky, *The Myths of Happiness. What Should Make You Happy, but Doesn't, What Shouldn't Make You Happy, but Does* (London: Penguin Press, 2013).

[20] Solomon. RL. (1980). The opponent process theory of acquired innovation: The costs of pleasure and the benefits of pain. American Psvchologist. 35. 691-7 t2. Frijda. N. 11. (1988). The laws of emotion. American Psychologist. 5. 349-358. Sonja Lyubomirsky, *The Myths of Happiness. What Should Make You Happy, but Doesn't, What Shouldn't Make You Happy, but Does* (London: Penguin Press, 2013).

[21] Ana Barrón López de Roda, et al. "Romantic beliefs and myths in Spain." The Spanish Journal of Psychology, 2(1), 64-73 (1999).

[22] Erich Fromm, *The Art of Loving* (New York: Harper Perennial, 1956/2006), 52.

[23] (Captain Corelli's Mandolin).

[24] Helen Fisher, "Biology: Your Brain in Love," *Time Magazine,* (Jan. 19, 2004).

[25] M. Scott Peck, *The Road Less Travelled* (Touchstone, 1988), *

[26] Baumeister, R. F. (1999). Passion, Intimacy, and Time: Passionate Love as a Function of Change in Intimacy Personality and Social Psychological Review, 3(1):49-67.

[27] (Nestler, 2001).

[28] As cited in Helen Fisher, The Drive to Love: The Neural Mechanism for Mate Selection in Robert J. Sternberg, Karin Weis Eds. *The New Psychology of Love* (New Haven: Yale University Press, 2008),103-104. Fisher summarizes, "any medication that changes chemical checks and balances is likely to alter an individual's courting, mating and parenting tactics."

[29] Gary Zukav, Soul Stories, (Free Press, 2000)

[30] Robert A. Johnson, *We: Understanding the Psychology of Romantic Love* (New York: HarperOne, 1985), 107-108.

[31] Italics mine. M. Scott Peck, *The Road Less Travelled* (Touchstone, 1988), 88, 119.

[32] Robert A. Johnson, *We: Understanding the Psychology of Romantic Love* (New York: HarperOne, 1985), 107-108.

[33] Lisa A. Neff and Benjamin R. Karney Compassionate Love in Early Marriage

[34] Dawn eden

[35] Lisa A. Neff and Benjamin R. Karney Compassionate Love in Early Marriage

[36] Lisa A. Neff and Benjamin R. KarneyTo Know You Is to Love You: The Implications of Global Adoration and Specific Accuracy for Marital Relationships. Journal of Personality and Social Psychology, Vol 88(3), Mar 2005, 480-497

[37] Robert A. Johnson, *We: Understanding the Psychology of Romantic Love* (New York: HarperOne, 1985), 107-108.

[38] Robert A. Johnson, *We: Understanding the Psychology of Romantic Love* (New York: HarperOne, 1985), 107-108.

[39] Robert A. Johnson, *We: Understanding the Psychology of Romantic Love* (New York: HarperOne, 1985), 199-200.

[40] Stanton Peele 1988. Fools for love: The romantic ideal, psychological theory and addictive love. In R.J. Sternberg & M.L. Barnes (Eds.), The psychology of love (pp. 159-190). New Haven, CT: Yale University Press. 182

[41] Erich Fromm, *The Art of Loving* (New York: Harper Perennial, 1956/2006), xvi.

[42] Patricia Noller, "What is this thing called love? Defining the love that supports marriage and family," Personal Relationships , 3(1), 1996, 105, 112

[43] Erich Fromm, *The Art of Loving* (New York: Harper Perennial, 1956/2006), 78.

[44] Robert A. Johnson, *We: Understanding the Psychology of Romantic Love* (New York: HarperOne, 1985), 102.

[45] Zygmunt Bauman, *Liquid Love: On the Frailty of Human Bonds* (Cambridge: Polity Press, 2003), 5.

[46] Barbara Dafoe Whitehead, *Why There Are No Good Men Left: The Romantic Plight of the New Single Woman* (New York: Broadway Books, 2003), 184.

[47] Robert A. Johnson, *We: Understanding the Psychology of Romantic Love* (New York: HarperOne, 1985), 103.

[48] Stephen Kendrick and Alex Kendrick, *The Love Dare* (Nashville: B&H Books, 2008), 66.

[49] M. Scott Peck in The Road Less Travelled (Touchstone, 1988), 156-157 - compares our relationship to feelings as that of a boss to employees: "The proper management of one's feelings clearly lies along a complex (and therefore not simple or easy) balanced middle path, requiring constant judgment and continuing adjustment. Here the owner treats his feelings (employees) with respect, nurturing them with good food, shelter and medical care, listening and responding to their voices, encouraging them, inquiring as to their health, yet also organizing them, limiting them, deciding clearly between them, redirecting them and teaching them, all the while leaving no doubt as to who is the boss."

[50] Stephen Kendrick and Alex Kendrick, *The Love Dare* (Nashville: B&H Books, 2008), vi.

[1] Lori Gottlieb, *Marry Him: The Case for Settling for Mr. Good Enough* (New York: New American Library, 2010), 31.

Chapter 10

[2] Cindy Hazan and Phillip Shaver, "Romantic Love Conceptualized as an Attachment Process," *Journal of Personality and Social Psychology*, 52(3), 511-524 (1987).

[3] Patricia Noller, "What is this thing called love? Defining the love that supports marriage and family," Personal Relationships , 3(1), 1996, 97

[4] Zygmunt Bauman, Liquid Love: On the Frailty of Human Bonds (Cambridge: Polity Press, 2003), 11.

[5] Zygmunt Bauman, Liquid Love: On the Frailty of Human Bonds (Cambridge: Polity Press, 2003), 6.

[6] J. Oke (1999). Love Comes Softly (Bethany House Publishers).

[7] Heads up for sensitive viewers - the film opens with a glimpse into an affair, but one that is tastefully done. Similar to Les Miserables, all the depictions of sensuality in the movie are purposive and teaching something. The Painted Veil (2006) Director: John Curran, Writers: Ron Nyswaner (screenplay), W. Somerset Maugham (novel)

[8] L..M. Montgomery, Anne of Avonlea (1909).

[9] Albert Y. Hsu, Singles at the Crossroads (Downer's Grove, IL: InterVarsity Press, 1997), 145.

[10] UCLA, "Here is what real commitment to your marriage means." ScienceDAily, (2012).

[11] Barbara Dafoe Whitehead and David Popenoe, "Who Wants To Marry A Soul Mate? New Survey Findings on Young Adults' Attitudes about Love and Marriage" The State of Our Unions (Rutgers University, The National Marriage Project, 2001).

[12] Gary Zukav, Soul Stories, (Free Press, 2000)

[13] Erich Fromm, The Art of Loving (New York: Harper Perennial, 1956/2006), 102, 119.

[14] Erich Fromm, The Art of Loving (New York: Harper Perennial, 1956/2006), 119.

[15] Robert A. Johnson, We: Understanding the Psychology of Romantic Love (New York: HarperOne, 1985), 151.

[16] Kay Hymowitz, Jason S. Carroll, W. Bradford Wilcox and Kelleen Kaye, "Knot Yet: The Benefits and Costs of Delayed Marriage in America," National Marriage Project at the University of Virginia (2013).

[17] Alex Williams "The End of Courtship?" New York Times (Jan 11, 2013).

[18] anonanon

[19] Wendy Walsh, The 30-day Love Detox (New York: Rodale, 2013), 39.

[20] Barbara Dafoe Whitehead, Why There Are No Good Men Left: The Romantic Plight of the New Single Woman (New York: Broadway Books, 2003), 4-5.

[21] Italics mine. Barbara Dafoe Whitehead, Why There Are No Good Men Left: The Romantic Plight of the New Single Woman (New York: Broadway Books, 2003), 124*

[22] Kay Hymowitz, Jason S. Carroll, W. Bradford Wilcox and Kelleen Kaye, "Knot Yet: The Benefits and Costs of Delayed Marriage in America," National Marriage Project at the University of Virginia (2013).

[23] Barbara Dafoe Whitehead and David Popenoe, "Who Wants To Marry A Soul Mate? New Survey Findings on Young Adults' Attitudes about Love and Marriage" The State of Our Unions (Rutgers University, The National Marriage Project, 2001).

[24] Barbara Dafoe Whitehead, *Why There Are No Good Men Left: The Romantic Plight of the New Single Woman* (New York: Broadway Books, 2003), 80.

[25] [As cited in Kay Hymowitz, Jason S. Carroll, W. Bradford Wilcox and Kelleen Kaye, "Knot Yet: The Benefits and Costs of Delayed Marriage in America," *National Marriage Project at the University of Virginia* (2013)] Original: Norval D. Glenn, Jeremy E. Uecker, and Robert W. B. Love, Jr., "Later First Marriage and Marital Success," Social Science Research 39 (September 2010): 787–800, 787.

[26] Kay Hymowitz, Jason S. Carroll, W. Bradford Wilcox and Kelleen Kaye, "Knot Yet: The Benefits and Costs of Delayed Marriage in America," *National Marriage Project at the University of Virginia* (2013).

[27] Kay Hymowitz, Jason S. Carroll, W. Bradford Wilcox and Kelleen Kaye, "Knot Yet: The Benefits and Costs of Delayed Marriage in America," *National Marriage Project at the University of Virginia* (2013).

[28] Pew Research Center "Childlessness up among all women: Down among women with advanced degrees." (June, 2010)

[29] Wendy Walsh, *The 30-day Love Detox* (New York: Rodale, 2013), 3, 19-20.

[30] Italics mine. Kay Hymowitz, Jason S. Carroll, W. Bradford Wilcox and Kelleen Kaye, "Knot Yet: The Benefits and Costs of Delayed Marriage in America," *National Marriage Project at the University of Virginia* (2013).

[31] Kay Hymowitz, Jason S. Carroll, W. Bradford Wilcox and Kelleen Kaye, "Knot Yet: The Benefits and Costs of Delayed Marriage in America," *National Marriage Project at the University of Virginia* (2013).

[31] Lori Gottlieb, *Marry Him: The Case for Settling for Mr. Good Enough* (New York: New American Library, 2010), 8.

Conclusion

[1] My estimate takes a 245/day estimated average multiplied by 7 days = 1715 - rounding down for a conservative estimate (For a more complete review of the data, see the response by Bobbie7-ga in 2002's Google Answers forum: http://answers.google.com/answers/threadview?id=58750).

[2] Richard Maisel, David Epston and Ali Borden, *Biting the hand that starves you: Inspiring resistance to anorexia/bulimia* (London: W. W. Norton & Company, 2005).

[3] Similar calls have been made for more work to surface and examine dominant 'scripts' surrounding beauty and physical intimacy, those same "unwritten and often unconscious rules" that guide our actions and lives [see Mark Regnerus and Jeremy Uecker, *Premarital Sex in a America: How Young Americans Meet, Mate and Think about Marrying*. (New York: Oxford University Press, 2011)].

[4] Brent D. Slife and Richard N. Williams, *What's behind the research? Discovering hidden assumptions in the behavioral sciences* (Thousand Oaks, CA: Sage, 1995).

[5] Lisa Appignanesi, *All about Love: Anatomy of an Unruly Emotion* (London: W. W. Norton & Company, 2011)

[6] M. Scott Peck, *The Road Less Travelled* (Touchstone, 1988), 107-108.

[7] Robert A. Johnson, *We: Understanding the Psychology of Romantic Love* (New York: HarperOne, 1985), 43-44.

[8] Robert A. Johnson, *We: Understanding the Psychology of Romantic Love* (New York: HarperOne, 1985), xiii, 98, 201.

[9] Lori Gottlieb, *Marry Him: The Case for Settling for Mr. Good Enough* (New York: New American Library, 2010), 24

[10] Charles Taylor, "Interpretation and the sciences of man." In C. Taylor, *Philosophical Papers Volume Two: Philosophy & Human Sciences* (New York, NY: Cambridge University Press, 1985); also J. Martin and J. Sugarman, "Interpreting human kinds: Beginnings of a hermeneutic psychology," *Theory & Psychology, 11* (2001).

[11] Wendy Shalit, *The Good Girl Revolution: Young Rebels with Self-Esteem and High Standards* (Ballantine Books, 2008) (www.thegoodgirlrevolution.com)

[12] (http://www.narrativeapproaches.com/)

[13] Naomi Wolf, *The Beauty Myth: How Images of Beauty are Used Against Women* (New York: Harper Perennial, 1992/2002), 277

[14] Solomon E. Asch, "Studies on independence and conformity: A minority of one against a unanimous majority," Psychological Monographs, 70 (1956); also S. Moscovici, E., Lage, M. and Naffrechoux, "Influence of a consistent minority on the responses of a majority in a color perception task," Sociometry, 32 (1969).

[15] Robert A. Johnson, *We: Understanding the Psychology of Romantic Love* (New York: HarperOne, 1985), xv, 156.

[16] Stephen Kendrick and Alex Kendrick, *The Love Dare* (Nashville: B&H Books, 2008), vi, vii.